W9-AHI-482

Moral Purity and Persecution in History

*

Moral Purity and Persecution in History

*

Barrington Moore, Jr.

PRINCETON UNIVERSITY PRESS

PRINCETON, NEW JERSEY

Library of Congress Cataloging-in-Publication Data

Moore, Barrington, 1913–
Moral purity and persecution in history / Barrington Moore, Jr.
p.   cm.
Includes bibliographical references and index.
ISBN 0-691-04920-3 (cloth : alk. paper)
1. Purity (Ethics)—History.   2. Persecution—History.   I. Title.
BJ1533.P97 M66   2000
323.44'2'09—dc21   99-048668

This book has been composed in Baskerville
The paper used in this publication meets the minimum requirements of
ANSI/NISO Z39.48-1992 (R1997) (*Permanence of Paper*)
http://pup.princeton.edu
Printed in the United States of America
1 3 5 7 9 10 8 6 4 2

TO MY STUDENTS

AND MY TEACHERS

ASHORE AND AFLOAT.

*

✻ *Contents* ✻

❋ *Preface* ❋

THIS BOOK examines when and why human beings kill and torture other human beings who, on account of their different religious, political, and economic ideas, appear as a threatening source of "pollution." What the polluting ideas were and are is of course a major aspect of the problem. They change over time. Yet this book is in no sense a work of intellectual or religious history. Instead it seeks to find out in what kind of a context this complex of ideas and action occurs. The complex itself one can easily recognize as a militant or very violent movement on behalf of moral purity. There is a good case for calling these movements against pollution attacks on moral *impurity*. Indeed, in this book moral impurity receives far more attention than its opposite. It is also rather more interesting. Still, impurity is impossible without purity.

That such movements have scarred the twentieth century and are well on the way to wounding the twenty-first is so obvious as scarcely to require comment. They were central to Fascism, Communism, and the imperial patriotism of Japan prior to its defeat in the Second World War. Since then they have cropped up, so far, in a relatively nonviolent form in the Christian right and in the Le Pen movement in France, and in a more violent form in Islamic movements and various others. These movements were the stimulus for writing this book. But they are not its topic.

Instead, this book seeks at least limited answers to two sets of general questions, those of time and place. How far back in time do we find a search for moral purity with a powerful component of violence? The Old Testament, the subject of the first chapter, is an obvious answer. The Old Testament records the invention of monotheism and the bloody struggles that accompanied its spread and establishment. Monotheism, in the straightforward sense of belief in one God and only one God, was apparently invented only once in human history. It necessarily implies a monopoly of grace and virtue to distinguish its adherents from surrounding and competing religions. The competition was, and has remained, fierce and cruel.

The first chapter will not review the whole of the Old Testament, though doing so could be quite rewarding. Instead, I will concentrate on the Pentateuch (the first five books of the Old Testament) and the prophet books Isaiah, Jeremiah with Lamentations of Jeremiah, and Ezekiel. The emphasis of this study is on the probable effects of moral doctrines, despite the very great difficulties in making such judgments. It is definitely not on ideas and doctrines for their own sake. For that reason, the text used will be the King James Version of the Holy Bible, which has had enormous resonance in the English-speaking world. In a few cases where a passage seemed both significant and obscure, I have resorted to the Revised Standard Version. Despite some disagreements I have also found much that is helpful in the extensive translation and commentary by Jacob Milgrom, *Leviticus 1–16* (New York, 1991).

The second chapter, on the French Wars of Religion, examines what took place when the institutional expression of monotheism for preceding centuries, the Roman Catholic Church, was fast losing its monopolistic control of purity in belief and behavior. There are many other possible ways to study what happened when the ideas in the Old Testament in modified form became the basis for political and religious action in western and central Europe. For example, one might choose the Crusades, with their bloody persecutions of the Jews. Going directly to sixteenth-century France has the advantage of displaying a conflict between two variants of monotheism, suggesting that any all-embracing system of beliefs will sooner or later be riven by heresy because of its claim to monopoly. A further and most important advantage is the existence of a crisis in the form of the Massacre of St. Bartholomew, which reveals in a lurid light the not-so-latent conflicts in French society.

In this book as a whole I have tried to make extensive use of primary sources. Even if obviously biased, they are the closest to the event and therefore often especially revealing. The Old Testament is, of course, a primary source. For the chapter on the French Wars of Religion, on the other hand, heavy reliance on primary sources would not be a counsel of perfection but of destruction. They are too few and too scattered. The all-important sequence of historical events has to emerge from secondary works. Therefore this chapter draws considerably on well-known classics of French historical writing such as the works of Imbart de la Tour, Michelet, and Lavisse, which frequently give direct quotations from major speeches of the day. Some local monographs are very enlightening as well. Still, the chapter does not entirely neglect primary evidence. It would have been impossible to write it without careful scrutiny of the writings of Jean Calvin, for example.

Chapter 3, on purity in the French Revolution, is our third historical sounding. By this time purity has ceased to be a religious concept and become a strictly secular one. At the same time it has retained its ethical exclusiveness: only the revolutionaries are pure. The rest of society becomes bit by bit a source of moral pollution that needs to be cut out and destroyed. In due course only *some* of the revolutionaries are pure. Not for the first nor the last time in human history, we see here orthodoxy creating heresy. But this was the first time the process took place within a secular framework. The secular aspect may have reached its apex under Fascism and Stalinism. Subsequently, religious, ethically exclusive, and often chauvinistic movements have grown up all over the world, by no means excluding the West.

The book changes its pace after the chapter on the secularization of moral purity in the French Revolution. In chapter 4 the focus shifts to a different question: Do large-scale movements on behalf of moral purity, roughly resembling those in Western civilization, appear under the main religions, Hinduism, Buddhism, and Confucianism, prior to substantial Western impact? Somewhat to the author's surprise, the answer turns out to be negative.

India presents an intriguing case for discussion. In pre-British times, and still to a great extent today, Indian society was organized around the principles of disgust and pollution expressed in caste hierarchies. But the bottom and most disgusting castes were not objects to be exterminated. Instead, they did the society's dirtiest and most strenuous work. Only in quite recent years has India managed to generate a movement for moral purity, with the usual punitive xenophobia and glorification. In assessing this negative conclusion, it is necessary to recall that the evidence from Asia prior to the European impact is long on religious and ethical doctrine and short on what ordinary people felt and did. Fortunately, modern scholarship is correcting this imbalance as far as the available sources permit.

This book's interpretation of historical materials takes the form of soundings into the available evidence. No other method is feasible with such a broad range of evidence, and a broad range is essential to asking when and where militant movements for moral purity occur. There is much more than intellectual parsimony behind this familiar and fruitful device. As many an anthropologist knows, cultural beliefs and deeply ingrained forms of social behavior appear most clearly in a crisis. To a widely varying degree, depending on the evidence, soundings make it possible to learn how the participants actually felt and behaved during a critical historical event. It is also possible to discover and use evidence that is inevitably left out of histories covering longer periods of time. There is an arbitrary element in any choice of sounding because the choice reflects an individual author's interests and knowledge. A reader might want to ask, "Why these soundings and not others?" The reply has a strong objective component: most of the chapters analyze the beginning of the religious conception of moral purity in Western civilization and subsequent crises on through the complete secularization.

When I begin a book, I have but the dimmest notion of how it might turn out. At most I have an issue and some ideas about the relevant evidence. The way to formulate the issue or issues and the meaning of the evidence comes to light gradually, literally sentence by sentence, in the course of working through the material. This procedure accounts for a certain ruminative style.

I try to show the reader the reasoning and evidence behind a thesis, and at times show contrary considerations as well. It seems to me that these supporting considerations and reservations are just as important, perhaps even more important, than high-flying general conclusions. Conclusions are in large measure a matter of luck. There is no guarantee that any particular body of historical facts will yield or support worthwhile general conclusions, though it helps to start with worthwhile issues.

Now that I have specified the main themes of *Moral Purity*, it may help readers to see what the book omits and why. A striking omission is the absence of any treatment of Islam, certainly one of the world's great religions, comparable to the discussion of, say, the Catholic-Huguenot conflicts in France, or even Confucianism. There are two reasons for this omission. Islam is a monotheistic religion owing a substantial debt to ancient Judaism. Since *Moral Purity* already has a great deal of material about monotheism and its permutations, there is little to be gained by piling up additional evidence from a source that was not historically independent from the others. The second reason is that I am less familiar with the literature of Islam than the other religious, intellectual, and social complexes analyzed in the book.

Nevertheless, it is necessary to at least call attention to the fact that Islam was, with one brief exception, not a persecuting religion during and after its great period of conquest and expansion, which reached its height around A.D. 730. For all the talk about "Islam or the Sword," the Islamic conquerors had to do what conquerors generally have to do if they seek more than an ephemeral victory: make a deal with the conquered. Mohammed's followers and successors did not require conversion. The payment of taxes came first. Without going into details, the treatment of subject peoples was relatively mild.

The absence of any discussion of Graeco-Roman civilization, and its transformation into a Christianity that begins with a message of love and forgiveness and turns into the horrors of the Inquisition, is the most striking omission. The reason for this omis-

xiii

sion is, in good measure, the opposite of unfamiliarity with the sources, as in the omission of Islam. In a sense I knew too much or, more precisely, enough to avoid a task that could have grossly unbalanced the book and swamped its author. The task was tempting because I know Greek and Latin well enough to use them as research tools. I also have some familiarity with the secondary literature. On the other hand, this is a theme that has attracted some very good minds ever since Gibbon. Even if in some cases they have reached diametrically opposite conclusions, I am not sure that I could have made a contribution commensurate with the time and effort invested. After all, the main differences between a polytheistic, mostly tolerant paganism and a Christianity that came to strive for militant purity are not exactly puzzling. If the main issues are widely understood, it would obviously be wiser to use a limited stock of energy on something else.

To avoid misapprehension, it is necessary to explain a different kind of omission. Since the emphasis is on collective fears of impurity and collective seeking for moral purity, there is hardly any discussion of those lone individuals who seek moral purification by abandoning civilization and going alone, or with a tiny group of companions, into the wilderness, often as hermits. It is worth mentioning here that the ideal of the hermit was a significant side-current in Buddhist theory and practice, as part of their very negative attitude towards life in civilization. Indeed, the hermit is a significant figure in many religions and quasi-religious movements. But *Moral Purity* is not a book about escapism. It is about explicit attempts to change a major moral climate.

One last comment on what is not in this book: references to all the latest scholarship on each subject discussed. There are, of course, numerous secondary works cited, because they were helpful, often indispensably so. But I have made no attempt at complete coverage. As other scholars facing the same situation have remarked in their prefaces, an attempt at complete coverage of scholarly works about, say, the Old Testament, would have left no time for careful reading of the Old Testament itself. The same applies to Jean Calvin, Maximilien Robespierre, Louis-Antoine Saint-Just, and Confucius. Secondary works are essential to place such figures in their historical context. Nevertheless, it is impossible to read all of them.

Inevitably, writing a book is to some degree a collective enterprise. It is a pleasant custom to express gratitude for assistance rendered and advice received. Yet, like many pleasant customs, it can on occasion become subject to distortion and exaggeration. Or so it seems to me. Half a page or more listing the names of every individual who has looked at the manuscript or had an interesting conversation with the author, and ending with the obligatory bow to spouse and offspring, impresses me as far too much of a good thing. A friend once said to me that such acknowledgments looked like a telephone directory. Can such an author ever say anything in print without first getting a guarantee of social support? As another friend once remarked to me, many authors today write as though they had a committee in their heads.

In keeping with these observations as well as objective facts, my thanks must be as brief as they are deeply felt. First my gratitude goes to Harvard University, and especially the ever helpful staff of Widener Library, with whom I have have been associated for almost half a century. Since 1948 the Russian Research Center (now the Davis Center for Russian Studies) has been my base at Harvard. For more than forty of these years the Center has warmly encouraged and enabled me to write about any topic I chose, whether it concerned Russia or not, a policy continued by the current director, Timothy J. Colton. I doubt that any other university in the world could or would have been so flexible and generous in providing marvelous resources for scholarship and intellectually curious students to teach. To Dr. Judith Vichniac I owe another large and pleasant debt. She was my last graduate student, and very soon became a family friend along with her husband and children. In recent years she has tried valiantly to restore in me the illusion that life is still worth living, and has been intermittently successful. With steadfast good humor Madeleine Wong computer-typed this manuscript, incorporating what must at times have seemed endless arbitrary revisions and corrections. For that she has earned this author's warm thanks.

Moral Purity and Persecution in History

*

Moral Purity and Impurity
in the Old Testament

THE ANALYSIS will begin with an interpretive survey of moral purity and impurity among the ancient Hebrews as revealed by the admonitions and prohibitions in the Old Testament. The reasons for choosing the Old Testament are obvious. It is no exaggeration to call it the moral template of Western civilization, even if departures from its moral code were numerous during the time it received written form and subsequently.

Wherever the notion of moral purity occurs—in Robespierre, the Hindu caste system, or the Old Testament—it is defined in the Hegelian manner by what purity is not, namely, impurity or pollution. Thus a morally pure person is free from moral pollution. The nature and sources of pollution vary a great deal in time and place.[1] Because pollution is the variable that defines purity, it becomes unavoidably the central subject of this study as a whole, not just the Old Testament.

The abundant sources of pollution reported in the Old Testament fall naturally into four distinguishable, if at some points overlapping, categories: (1) sexual prohibitions, (2) idolatry, (3) dietary restrictions, and (4) unclean objects, such as blood and corpses. Insofar as the violation of any prohibition in this series appears as a violation of the will of God (God's will being the only justification for the prohibition), it appears that for the ancient Hebrew religious authorities such acts were very serious moral failures. When one gets down to cases, this conclusion seems rather odd. Hence this aspect will require fuller discussion after examining the details. We shall take up each of the four forms of pollution, which frequently intertwine, in turn.

SEXUAL PROHIBITIONS AND IDOLATRY

Beginning with sex, the first point worth noticing is its connection with apparently attractive foreign practices and with idolatry, which is, if anything, even more seductive. The religious authorities made strenuous, though hardly successful, efforts to prohibit these presumably attractive sexual practices as foreign, polluting, and idolatrous. These prohibitions in turn sought to prevent the ancient Hebrews from being culturally absorbed by the peoples they had conquered and thereby in danger of losing their religious identity. Although if the religious authorities lost many moral skirmishes over sexual behavior, they did win the big battle for a separate identity.

At the beginning of a long list of sexual prohibitions in Leviticus 18, God in verse 3 enjoins the children of Israel to avoid the "doings of the land of Egypt, wherein ye dwelt" and "the doings of the land of Canaan, whither I bring you." This prohibition brings to mind the widespread human (or merely male?) tendency to attribute forbidden yet tempting sexual practices to neighboring foreigners. Following the list of sexual practices, God makes it clear that these acts are forms of pollution engaged in by foreigners. Lev. 18:24 tells the children of Israel not to "defile" themselves in these ways, "for in all these the nations are defiled which I cast out before you."

The connection between sexual attraction and idolatry appears in a brief and obscure passage, Lev. 20:1–5, recounting the death penalty for either Israelite or stranger who gives "any of his seed unto Molech." Molech was a Canaanite god of fire to whom children were sacrificed. Mention of his worship by the children of Israel recurs in other parts of the Bible. In the Pentateuch I have found only one other explicit reference to the attractiveness of idolatry. It is a powerful and dramatic passage (Deut. 13:6–12), though with no more than the faintest hint of sexuality. If, among other relatives, "the wife of thy bosom or thy friend . . . of thine own soul, entice thee secretly, saying, Let us go and serve other gods," the child of Israel was of course expected to refuse. That was the least of his obligations. "Thou shalt surely kill him [the tempter]; thine hand shall be first upon him to put him to death. . . . thou shalt stone him with stones that he die": the horrible severity of the punishment testifies to the presumed strength of the temptation. Throughout the discussion of the penalty the tempter is assumed to be a male friend, even though the introduction raises the possibility of a wife and other female relatives. In the writings of the prophets, to which we now turn briefly, the temptation of idolatry comes from a sexually attractive woman whose morals could stand improvement.

Immediately after his famous objection to grinding the faces of the poor (Is. 3:15), the prophet Isaiah lets off a blast against Jerusalem's attractive women of loose morals (Is. 3:16–24). This extended fulmination must be close to the acme of antisexual oratory in world literature. After describing the women's attractions in loving detail, Isaiah threatens that their "sweet smell" would turn to "stink," and their beauty to burning, as desolation overcame the city. However, this text contains no specific mention of pollution. Pollution is there only to the extent of a general belief among religious authorities that forbidden sexual behavior is polluting. Isaiah does emphasize that such acts are a mortal threat to Jerusalem, but no more.

In Jeremiah, pollution is explicitly linked with sexual misbehavior. As in the passage just cited from Isaiah, Jeremiah uses the device of treating Jerusalem as an attractive woman. Early on in the text (Jer. 2:23), God addresses her thus: "How canst thou say I am not polluted, I have not gone after Baalim [deities of Canaan]." Again, at Jer. 3:1–2, she is accused of playing the harlot with many lovers and polluting the land with her whoredoms and wickedness. A list of sins occurs at Jer. 7:9 that presumably summarizes contemporary religious beliefs about the worst forms of evil behavior. The list is brief: theft, murder, adultery, false swearing, and idolatry. In light of the many forms of sexual behavior prohibited elsewhere in the Old Testament, to be discussed shortly, the limitation here to adultery is striking.

Toward the close of Jeremiah there is a revealing passage (Jer. 44:15–19) on the practice of idolatry that suggests what God's advocates were up against. Too long for quotation or even as a satisfactory précis, here are the main points. Jeremiah addressed a huge crowd of idolators, both men and women. But only the women burned incense to other gods, though the men knew about it. The crowd supposedly told Jeremiah that they would continue to burn incense to the queen of heaven and pour drink offerings to her as their fathers, kings, and princes had done: "For then we had plenty of victuals, and were well and saw no evil." But after the idolaters had ceased burning incense and pouring drink offerings for the queen, they suffered want of all things and were consumed by the sword and by famine. Jeremiah's reply was (1) to blame the idolatry for their current misfortune and (2) to threaten more thorough destruction (Jer. 44:20–29). That was consistent with Jeremiah's general remedy for or reaction to idolatry: nearly total slaughter and destruction (Jer. 46:10, 48:10).

The connections among sexual attractiveness, idolatry, and general wickedness receive even more emphasis in Ezekiel. Chapter 23 is an extended allegory of the doings of two women representing Samaria and Jerusalem. Their "whoredoms" receive detailed attention that includes the pressing of their breasts and bruising the teats of their virginity (Ezek. 23:3, 21). One of them took as lovers Assyrians "clothed with blue, . . . all of them desirable young men, horsemen riding upon horses" (Ezek. 23:5–6). God threatens to destroy them because they are "polluted with [heathen] idols" (Ezek. 23:30). The allegory closes, not surprisingly, with God's order to have them stoned to death. "Thus I will cause lewdness to cease out of the land," God declares, "that all women may be taught not to do after your lewdness" (Ezek. 23:47–48). Ezekiel 16 is a very similar sexual metaphor for religious and political issues. Once again the severity of the threatened penalties strongly suggests an anticipation that lewdness would not be easy to eradicate.

Fantasies about the sexual attractiveness of idolatry occupied much of the imagination of religiously active ancient Hebrews.

For them it was a major form of moral impurity. However, idolatry was not the only aspect of sexual immorality that concerned them. Before turning to a consideration of the other aspects, it will be well to consider two major sexual prohibitions that do not have any apparent connection with conceptions of impurity or pollution.

Both of these occur in the Ten Commandments (Ezek. 20: 2–17; Deut. 5:6–21). One is the prohibition on adultery. The other is the prohibition on coveting one's neighbor's wife. For none of the Ten Commandments is any special sanction or penalty for disobedience mentioned.[2] That is true of other prohibitions to be discussed shortly. That God decreed them is presumably enough. In the case of the Ten Commandments the awe surrounding their transmission to Moses (Ezek. 31:18; 32:15–19; 34:1–28) could be taken to preclude any discussion on this occasion of penalties including pollution. Yet the absence of any notion of pollution connected with these prohibitions I find quite puzzling. Perhaps the explanation lies in the shock of the occasion together with the probability that penalties were taken for granted. Think of the example of murder, also of course prohibited here. When it occurs it usually produces a shock as the crime becomes known. In ancient societies generally, the person who sheds blood is polluted. But it would be somewhat ridiculous to have a special decree announcing that murder leads to moral impurity. People know that anyway. From that point of view violation of *any* of the Ten Commandments is a serious moral evil, because it is a direct flouting of God's will about a major issue. That simple statement, I suspect, accounts for the absence of explicit mention of pollution in connection with the Ten Commandments.

The ancient Hebrews had a long, complex series of ordinances against "uncovering the nakedness" of specific categories of women. Each category specifies one or more women who were in a potentially incestuous relationship with the male onlooker. To be more precise, the existence of a rule against seeing a certain woman naked indicates that the ancient Hebrews believed there was a potentially incestuous hazard. Characteristically the ancient Hebrews tried to build moral ramparts or outworks against serious temptation by prohibiting not only the tempting act but even awareness of the temptation.

There are two similar but not identical lists of these prohibitions, Lev. 18:6–20 and 20:17–21, which require no summary here. The first list contains no penalties that would throw light on ancient Hebrew moral feelings, except for the crucial one that these acts were "abominations" (Lev. 18:29), the standard epithet for any act felt to be both disgusting and morally repulsive. The second list has a graded list of penalties, starting with execution, which applied to most examples, passing through "cutting off from among the people," to rather light penalties. If a man lies with his uncle's wife, both will have sinned and die childless. If a man takes his brother's wife, it is an unclean act and both of them will be childless (Lev. 20:20–21). Is it out of the question that in both cases the partners in a morally impure act of passion would prefer to be childless?

Mixed in with the rules about nakedness are two prohibitions on perversions. One prohibits homosexuality in the strict sense of the word: sexual relations between males. This is an abomination (Lev. 18:22). There is no mention of lesbianism. Two possible explanations for this odd omission come to mind. Conceivably the male religious authorities who created this legislation didn't even know about its existence. Or else they were so terrified at the prospect of female joys without the male contribution that they did not even call attention to lesbianism by passing an ordinance against it. Some variant of the first explanation seems more likely. If the authorities had spoken about it, we can be sure they would have called it an abomination.

The second prohibition is against intercourse with a beast (Lev. 18:23).[3] It applies to both men and women and is characterized as "confusion," a form of ignoring proper boundaries and mixing things that ought not to be mixed, which received astonishing emphasis in ancient Hebrew dietary restrictions. To a modern it may seem odd that sexual intercourse with an animal is equated with a dietary rule. But for the ancient Hebrews, as well as some of their successors, both prohibitions carried and still carry a high moral charge.

We may close this limited survey of sex and moral impurity with a brief review of the varying penalties and conceptions of impurity connected with fornication. Marital sex for the sake of procreation, be it noted at the start, received from God frequent and strong endorsement in the repeated injunction to be fruitful and multiply. I have not noticed in the Old Testament, with the curious exception of the Song of Solomon, any endorsement of what we now call recreational sex. Explicit doubts and reservations about such pleasures evidently had to await the coming of Christianity. The same is true for masturbation. The one example mentioned in the Old Testament, that of Omar, who refused intercourse with his brother's wife (Gen. 38:8–10), is too special to permit any general inferences. The most one can guess is that the silence of the Old Testament about masturbation does not imply consent.

According to Lev. 19:20–22 fornication with a bondmaid betrothed to a husband was a sin. However, as might be expected in an ancient patriarchal society, the penalty was vastly lighter than the death penalty for ordinary adultery. The bondmaid was not to be given her freedom. Instead of being put to death she was to be scourged: "because she was not free." As for the man, he was required to bring a ram to the door of the tabernacle as a trespass offering for God. The priest would then make atonement for him before God for his sin, and the sin would be forgiven. In other words, if the man had enough property to spare a ram, for him there was nothing to the whole business. The poor girl at least got off with her life, though she was severely punished and probably lost her husband-to-be.

The famous episode of Joseph refusing an invitation to a sexual encounter issued by the wife of his Egyptian master, Potiphar, is not very enlightening for the purpose at hand. Nevertheless, it requires mention because it is so famous. Joseph bases his refusal on loyalty to a master who has trusted him and gives

9

him much responsibility and authority. "How then," said Joseph to the seducing wife, "can I do this great wickedness, and sin against God?" (Gen. 39:9). Joseph's objection states a straightforward moral position. Its stress on disloyalty resonates beyond his own age and culture to make the tale so famous. For the effect, God is hardly necessary.

The last episode to be discussed here is the "defilement" of Dinah (Gen. 34). The story indicates that if a presentable young man had intercourse with a presentable young Hebrew woman and, falling in love, asked the woman's father for her hand in marriage, the request might be happily granted. All that would be quite ordinary if the young man were another Hebrew. If he were a foreigner, even of high status, as is the case in this episode here, matters could turn out very differently. As strangers with a strange religion and conquerors in a new land, the Hebrews were fiercely endogamous, or at least tried to be.

Dinah was the daughter of Jacob, the famous Hebrew patriarch. When Shechem, son of a prince of the country, "saw her, he took her, and lay with her and defiled her." Then Shechem asked his father to "get the damsel to wife." The father took counsel with Jacob, who kept quiet until his sons came in from the fields. When they arrived, they were very angry at Shechem. To abbreviate the rest of the story, Jacob's son deceived Shechem and his father by pretending to agree to their generous offer of a dowry and future intermarriage on condition that all males in Shechem's city be circumcised. Shechem and his father agreed to the condition, whereat two of Dinah's brothers took their swords and killed all the males in Shechem's city. At this point the tale becomes quite hard to believe, though the attitudes it reveals remain very credible. After the slaughter the two brothers despoiled the city, taking all the sheep, oxen, asses, and other property, even the wives, whom they took captive. Then the story becomes very believable once more. Jacob angrily told the two murderous brothers of Dinah that they had made him "stink among the inhabitants of the land" (pollution again), who greatly outnumbered him and would slay him and destroy his house. To this outburst the two brothers responded with a reference to their sister's honor: "And they said, should he deal with our sister as with a harlot?" This obligation to avenge defilement here overrides ordinary prudence. Furthermore, vengeance as legitimate aggression can yield tremendous pleasure, especially if it takes the form of a defense of moral purity.

We turn now to idolatry as impurity. Since we have already had occasion to discuss idolatry at some length in connection with its erotic attractiveness, its other features need not detain us long. The classic statement about the dangers of idolatry for religious and hence moral purity occurs in Deut. 13:13–18. According to God's ordinances as reported here, if there is a rumor about idolatry in a city given by God to the Hebrews, and upon diligent inquiry the rumor turns out to be true, then "Thou shalt surely smite the inhabitants of that city with the edge of the sword, destroying it utterly. . . . And thou shalt gather all the spoils of it unto the midst of the street thereof, and shall burn with fire the city, and all the spoil thereof every whit." An earlier passage, Deut. 12:31, refers to idolatry as an abomination, the epithet commonly applied to polluted or polluting objects. Thus this text is a sinister justification of slaughter for the sake of moral purity.

The best-known episode of idolatry is that of the golden calf (Exod. 32). Actually there are two more episodes (I Kings 12: 26–32; Hos. 8:5–6). Since the latter two add nothing from the point of view of this inquiry, a brief comment on the first one will suffice. When Moses disappeared for a time to consult with God, the people of Israel "gathered themselves together" to request Aaron, Moses' brother and right-hand man, "to make us gods, which shall go before us," because they did not know what had become of Moses (Exod. 32:1). In other words, the demand for idols similar to those used by neighboring peoples surfaced as soon as Moses disappeared. Evidently Moses—or the Hebrew religious authorities generally—did not enjoy the confidence of the people, who were drawn to the indigenous deities and tried to imitate them. Naturally God became furious. We can

11

pass over Moses' limited success in placating his anger (Exod. 32:7–14) to note God's punishment: the sons of Levi put to the sword some three thousand men, after which God sent a plague on the people of Israel (Exod. 32:28–35). In the whole episode there is only a hint of pollution, when God says that the people "have corrupted themselves." For the rest the emphasis is on the "great sin" (Exod. 32:31) that the people have committed. As in the preceding case, the stress here is on slaughter in defense of religious purity. A monotheistic invention that has been with us for centuries.

DIETARY RESTRICTIONS AND UNCLEAN OBJECTS

We may turn now to the numerous and much discussed notions of pollution from a variety of objects that may enter the human body, be excreted by the body, or otherwise come in contact with it. Very many human societies, literate and nonliterate, have had numerous rules about pollution and the human body.[4]

However, so far as I am aware, no other society has elaborated the ideas and practices connected with pollution to anything like the extent found amongst the ancient Hebrews. The explanation may lie in the struggle to establish monotheism in a sea of hostile pagan societies. As Mary Douglas has pointed out in *Purity and Danger*, elaborate rules, especially dietary rules, helped the ancient Hebrews preserve their distinctive identity, the justification for their existence.[5] Recently a distinguished Biblical scholar, Jacob Milgrom, has pointed out that the advent of monotheism meant the end of all the little gods and near gods that occasionally helped but more often hurt the ordinary mortals in the surrounding pagan societies.[6] In such societies petty gods often have specific functions, both damaging and helpful, much like an array of over-the-counter remedies. In comparison with highly accessible pagan threats and remedies, the new monotheistic God was not only unapproachable. He was terrifying. Though Milgrom might vehemently reject this inference, the situation makes it seem highly likely that the ancient Hebrew rules about pollution were in many cases taken over from pagan practices, especially forms of propitiation. Doing that would have enabled Hebrew priestly authorities to deflect the competitive threat of paganism, a device standard for conquering rulers. Meanwhile the pagan deity disappeared in the transfer as it became a practice sanctioned by an ordinance of the new God.

The Book of Leviticus presents a long series of divine ordinances about what is unclean. Their violation is clearly a moral lapse that requires expiation. If a person touches the "carcass of an unclean beast . . . or unclean creeping things," even unintentionally, "he shall also be unclean and *guilty*" (Lev. 5:2, emphasis added). There follows his "trespass offering unto the Lord for his sin" in the form of a choice of animals for sacrifice (Lev. 5:6–7). The priest then makes an atonement for him, which results in forgiveness (Lev. 5:13).[7] According to a later passage, Lev. 7:21, there is no forgiveness for slightly different violations: touching "the uncleanness of man" and eating "of the flesh of the sacrifice of peace offerings which pertain unto the Lord." The person who does that "shall be cut off from his people." Presumably this frequently mentioned penalty amounts to internal ostracism. It apparently means that no one may have any contact with such a guilty person, a very severe penalty in a society heavily dependent on mutual cooperation.

Chapter 10 of Leviticus presents rules about sacrifice and the tabernacle. It begins with a brief tale about the sons of Aaron, who offered a sacrifice to God with a strange fire and incense, which God had not commanded. For this pagan-seeming sacrifice God killed them with fire. (Lev. 10:1–2). There follow certain actions that have to do with the sanctity of the tabernacle. Mourners for the dead sons of Aaron were not to go out of the tabernacle, because the anointing oil of the Lord was upon them and they would die (Lev. 10:7). As indicated here and in numerous other passages, direct contact with God could be lethal, and the tabernacle had to be kept pure at all costs. The people obeyed this instruction. The passage continues with a

13

series of instructions and miscellaneous ordinances issued directly by God to Aaron for the children of Israel. The most general and the most striking is "that ye may put difference between holy and unholy and between unclean and clean" (Lev. 10:10).

The meaning of this famous passage is far from obvious. At first glance it appears that ancient Hebrew religious authorities were working their way towards a distinction between pollution and the unholy. Unholy things might be profane in the sense of everyday, unconsecrated, essentially neutral morally, but very much out of place in a sanctified area. There is some evidence in support of this interpretation. Thus no stranger could "eat of the holy thing." The same rule applied to the daughter of a priest if she were married to a stranger (Lev. 22:10–12). Strangers had a special and respected status in ancient Israel. There was nothing polluting about them, at least not in religious theory. Popular attitudes may have differed.

If there was a movement towards developing a concept of the profane yet morally neutral, it did not get far. The main concern about holiness was fear lest it be contaminated by impure and disgusting objects.[8] Elsewhere Milgrom notes more specifically that "Israel must not contaminate itself by ingesting land swarmers because holiness, the goal it must seek, cannot coexist with impurity."[9]

Thus impurity remains the decisive threat, and certainly a moral one, because it is a threat to holiness. Holiness may not have been even remotely the dominant social objective of all the children of Israel. But the clearly dominant priests of that time saw it as a divine objective.

Returning to this rich chapter 10 of Leviticus, a key source on holiness and contamination, we learn in verses 12–13 that Moses instructed Aaron and his two remaining sons to eat the meat offering of the sacrifices to the Lord and "eat it without leaven beside the altar: for it is most holy." They were to eat "in the holy place." This concrete example shows that holy can mean sanctified to God, therefore having special qualities, including dangerous ones, and requiring special treatment. Since religion *was* morality for the ancient Hebrews, unlike the ancient Greeks and other ancient peoples, the special treatment was a moral obligation. As we have seen, there was a great deal of popular resistance to the acceptance of the new moral obligations. The discussion of the rules governing the sacrifice continues with the report that Moses "diligently sought the goat of the sin offering," only to discover that it was burnt. Thereupon Moses became angry with the sons of Aaron in charge of the sacrifice, scolding them by asking why they had not eaten the sin offering in the holy place after "God hath given it to you to bear the inequity of the congregation, to make atonement for them before the Lord" (Lev. 10: 16–17). The failure to carry out the sacrifice properly is less important for present purposes than the purpose of the sacrifice. The sacrificed goat that was to bear the iniquity of the congregation is, of course, a device for making guilt bearable. Just about every human society has such devices, reflecting a very widespread human necessity. The ancient Hebrew goat sacrifice, about which there is more detail in Leviticus 16, has entered the English language as "scapegoat," presumably because two goats were chosen, according to Lev. 16:8–10, one sacrificed and one allowed to escape into the wilderness to make atonement with God. Though mechanisms like this to make morality tolerable are common ones in human societies, efforts to create and intensify guilt feelings also occur. Religion can create guilt and then "cure" it. There is a good deal of evidence that this process was taking place among the ancient Hebrews. When we come to the Calvinists, who modeled themselves on the ancient Hebrews, the process of creating or at least recreating guilt will become obvious. Whether the Calvinists had a cure is less clear.

Following the rules about sacrifices and sin offerings come the famous and still puzzling—and still widely observed—rules about what one may eat, and more important, what one may not eat because it is unclean (Lev. 11; also Deut. 14). For a long time scholars have debated whether the prohibitions are essentially arbitrary or display some underlying order and rationality.[10] For the purpose of this inquiry it is unnecessary to solve this puzzle. We are merely interested in whether the prohibitions as they stand constituted a set of divine commands and therefore moral ordinances for the children of Israel. It is plain that in the course of time they became moral ordinances, if they were not such at the start. The prophet Ezekiel (fl. 600 B.C.) told God that his soul was "not polluted" because he had adhered to the dietary restrictions.

To probe a trifle further, the dietary restrictions resemble a set of avoidance rules that at one time or another have made their appearance in different societies all over the world.[11] Societies make avoidance rules in order to keep people away from something thought to be dangerous, such as incest, disease, or many other threats. In nonliterate societies, and by no means only those, the threat is perceived as the result of having offended a ghost, failed to propitiate an evil spirit, or still some other malevolent aspect of the environment. The remedy then is to prohibit contact with what appears to be the source of danger. From graduate-school days the writer still recalls the case of an isolated society where a plague broke out shortly after a camel appeared there for the very first time. The society responded by prohibiting any more visits by camels. Justification for avoidance rules thus frequently displays *post hoc ergo propter hoc* logic along with a strong emphasis on propitiation. In the case of the ancient Hebrew dietary rules, under the influence of time and monotheism, the logic has vanished to become God's will. The element of propitiation remains and is indeed overriding. Demons and ghosts have disappeared. Hence God is responsible—though not completely—for disaster as well as good fortune. These changes intensify the need to propitiate God. Despite a visible tendency towards making divine ordinances ethical and moral in the sense of promoting social welfare, the line between magic and morality is at times very hard to discern.

Mixed in with divine ordinances about forbidden and acceptable foods and the proper treatment of skin disease are some ordinances against mingling or the disregard for supposedly natural boundaries, natural in this case meaning created by God. Thus, according to Lev. 19:19, the Israelites were forbidden to let

16

diverse kinds of cattle interbreed, to sow their fields with mixed seeds, or to wear a garment made of mixed linen and wool. The prohibitions are preceded by God's statement "Ye shall keep my statutes," indicating that their violation was a serious sin.

A similar divine ordinance against mingling occurs in Lev. 18:23, which prohibits both men and women from having sexual intercourse with a beast. For a man it is called a defilement, for a woman a perversion. Mary Douglas, in *Purity and Danger,* reports that the word "perversion" is a mistranslation of *tebhel,* which means mixing or confusion.

Nearly all moderns would draw a sharp moral distinction between bestiality and, say, wearing a sweater made half of wool and half of polyester. (The grounds for a moral revulsion against bestiality present a separate issue. Here it is enough to claim the revulsion exists.) But the apparent absence of any distinction is the important point for our purposes. Leviticus and Deuteronomy are mainly compilations of divine ordinances, presented as coming directly from God. All sorts of prohibitions reflecting what are for us wildly different moral concerns are jumbled together. Following the prohibition on mixing linen and wool come in the same chapter (1) a prohibition on rounding the corners of their heads and marring the corners of their beards (Lev. 19:27) and next (2) a prohibition on prostituting one's daughter (Lev. 19:29).

Mary Douglas, in *Purity and Danger,* tries to make sense of the dietary restrictions and the prohibitions on mingling through the ancient Hebrew concept of holiness. Milgrom's thesis in *Leviticus 1–16* is similar. As I read them, Douglas and Milgrom are telling us that the priests of those days purported to be moral perfectionists engaged in the effort to make of Israel a morally and religiously perfect world, that is, a holy one. Hence the attention to matters that seem so utterly trivial today. Hence the demand that apparent divisions in God's creation—between humans and beasts, those affected by incest and adultery, as well as those between different kinds of cattle, seed, and cloth—must at all costs remain firm and unbreached.

So far as I can see, the concept of holiness does help to bring out an intelligible order in these divine ordinances. With respect and admiration for these scholars I will, however, offer what may be a much shorter and less perilous route to a similar conclusion. The attempt to find some sort of order or rationale to these ordinances may be a waste of time, a rather ethnocentric one at that. By that reasoning it may be worse than a waste of time, it may be a serious mistake. Instead, we might do better by taking the utter arbitrariness and lack of apparent reason for these ordinances as a major ethnographic fact about ancient Hebrew society. Doing that avoids straining the evidence with numerous questionable inferences. It also enables us to see that the first monotheistic God was at least as arbitrary as some of his polytheistic predecessors, and rather more so than many. Why the arbitrariness? The answer is rather simple. Power that is not used ceases to be recognized as power. As the Old Testament shows repeatedly, the ancient Hebrews had a siege mentality. They needed a God who could get results, even if they were often far from contented with the results. To the priests, presumably, that didn't matter. They wanted a frightened, obedient population. This combination of circumstances pushed in the direction of making all areas of life, from sex to sowing the fields, subject to divine ordinance. Every act was being made a matter of religious concern. The line between sacred and profane was becoming blurred, if indeed the priests had ever recognized one. In this sense there truly was pressure to become a godly or holy society, whose transgressors were religiously and morally impure.

Having discussed what may not go into the human body in the form of food and not go on it in the form of mixed fabrics, we can pass rapidly over what comes out of it in sickness and in health. Since most of these rules have parallels in numerous other societies, we shall linger only over those relevant to the central theme of this inquiry.

The end of life is, of course, death. The uncleanness of corpses and necessary purification rites appear in Num. 19: 11–22. The impurities of childbirth are recounted in Lev. 12.

Hebrew religious authorities displayed intense interest in the impurities of bodily secretions, especially the normal and pathological ones of males. They are described and analyzed in Lev. 15 with extended commentary in Milgrom (*Leviticus 1–16,* 763–768, 902–1009), which also treats childbirth and menstruation. I have come upon no references to feces, for which there is no reference in Milgrom's index of subjects. This apparent absence is rather curious, since just about every known human society has a system of toilet training that reveals adult feelings about the impurity of feces. Human blood, on the other hand, was the object of special attention when it had been shed by violent means. According to Num. 35:33, blood defiled the land. Further: "the land cannot be cleansed of the blood that is shed therein, but by the blood of him that shed it." Here we encounter the ethic of the traditional blood feud. In the case of coming upon the body of a man lying in the field and the murderer unknown, there was a special ritual to drive away "the guilt of innocent blood from among you" (Deut. 21:1–9, quotation from verse 9). The elders of the city nearest the dead body were to wash their hands over a beheaded heifer and say, "Our hands have not shed this blood, neither have our eyes seen it" (verse 8). Then came an appeal to God to "lay not innocent blood" to the charge of the people of Israel. Then they were to forgive the blood (verse 8), and, as mentioned at the start, the guilt of innocent blood would depart. The message of this tale appears to be thus: there has been a murder and therefore blood-guilt-threatening pollution. Since it is impossible to find the murderer, only God, properly approached, can remove the blood. The magical element is evident and powerful throughout the tale. But the element of divine approval and potential disapproval, which human specialists must seek, makes the tale a moral one.[12]

We may now turn to the treatment of leprosy, reported in detail in Lev. 14–15. For this inquiry the account is important for what it reveals about conceptions of moral responsibilities. The first problem, however, is one of identification. According to

19

Milgrom (*Leviticus 1–16*, 816–817), the disease called leprosy in Leviticus and other passages in the Old Testament is not leprosy at all. Instead, it is some strange skin disease that modern medicine is unable to identify completely. Milgrom calls it scale disease, after some of the symptoms. For the sake of accuracy I will adopt his terms. For our purposes precise identification is of small moment. We need to know how it was treated and especially if the treatment had a moral component.

The priest was responsible for determining whether or not a person showing suspicious symptoms actually had the scale disease. His diagnosis was elaborate and interesting but cannot detain us here. Two possible outcomes appear in the text.

One is that the patient's affliction turns out to be incurable, according to the priest's diagnosis. In that case the victim of scale was treated quite literally like an outcaste, in a way that recalls the treatment of the leper for many centuries. He—only a man is mentioned at this point—had to rend his clothes, bare his head, cover his upper lip, and cry, "Unclean, unclean." As long as he had the plague he would be defiled and must dwell alone outside the camp (Lev. 13:45–46). This penalty is not to be taken as mainly a primitive form of quarantine before the advent of the germ theory of disease. The most one can claim on these lines is that the penalty might be based on an avoidance rule similar to those discussed above. Both explanations miss the main point. Scale disease is a moral defect, indeed, moral pollution (as the expressions unclean and defilement show). The plague comes from God (Lev. 14:33). A moral failing requires a moral penalty. To judge from these books of the Old Testament, the ancient Hebrews at this time lacked any other way of thinking about these matters. With the end of polytheistic demons as causes of sickness and misfortunes, the only possible explanation became a moral one: failure to obey God's will. To label a person as unclean for an indefinite future and expel such a person from the community, cutting the individual off from most if not all social supports, was about as severe a moral penalty as possible under the conditions of those days. Only execution would have been more severe, and might have seemed preferable to some long-term victims.

The second outcome of scale disease appears to be some sort of spontaneous cure or at least well-established remission. It does not appear that the priest played any role in the cure. According to the text, the man (again only males) is to be brought to the priest, whereas the priest is expected to go out of the camp and make sure the man is really healed of the plague (Lev. 14:2–4). The task of the priest is to make the man clean and present him before God (Lev. 14:11). As I understand the passage, the priest is not to clean him in the sense of cure him, because that has already happened. Instead the priest is expected to take charge of a ceremony that will be a rite of passage to certify that the man has passed from the stage of being unclean and defiled to the stage of being clean and acceptable to God. Hence the ceremony includes the usual trespass offering and sin offering, and atonement (Lev. 14:11–19).

To sum up provisionally, there was a heavy moral penalty for coming down with scale disease and a correspondingly great reward for getting cured. In these divine ordinances there is no sign that the human individual played any role in getting sick or well. There were powerful moral imperatives and incentives to recover.[13] But there was no such thing as individual moral responsibility: God made one sick. Getting well was just mysterious. God does not appear to have any connection with remission or recovery.

The absence of moral responsibility, combined with a strong sense of moral failure curable by religious sacrifice, may seem inconsistent to at least some late-twentieth-century ways of thinking. But it is quite consistent with the concept of an omnipotent God. It also renders comprehensible the most curious items in the long discussion of scale disease: what to do about a house that comes down with this malady (Lev. 14:33–57).

Most modern householders would probably recognize both what the King James Bible (Lev. 14:44) calls "fretting leprosy" and Milgrom (*Leviticus 1–16*, 829) translates as "malignant fungus" as plain, ordinary mildew, a familiar result of warmth, dampness, and inadequate ventilation. The ancient treatment of a home with scale is similar to that for humans. As with humans, the priest is in charge of the whole operation. First there is an attempt to get rid of the plague by getting rid of infected parts, scraping, and replastering. If that does not work, the house has to be destroyed. If, on the other hand, the priest finds that the plague has not spread, he undertakes a sacrifice, as in the case of a human who appears cured. However, the sacrifice in the case of the house is different. The essential elements in this sacrifice are these. The priest takes two birds. He kills one and uses its blood in a ceremonial cleansing of the house, sprinkling it seven times. The living bird, on the other hand, he lets go "out of the city into the open fields, and makes an atonement for the house: and it shall be clean" (Lev. 14:53). The offering of an atonement indicates that a house, like a human, could be unclean in a sinful sense. Four verses later the discussion of scale disease comes to an end: "To teach when it is unclean and when it is clean: this is the law of leprosy [scale disease]." It is the uncleanness that matters and that is sent by God.

CONCLUSION

In concluding this chapter it is appropriate to raise once more the vexing question of whether or not the very miscellaneous collection of divine ordinances in Leviticus and Deuteronomy really have anything to do with moral purity and impurity. *Pace* Milgrom, did the ancient Hebrews really think in terms of morality and immorality? It is obvious that they did think in terms of ritual and religious impurity as well as ritual and religious techniques of purification. But that is not quite the same thing as morality. Unless I have missed something, the word "moral" or an equivalent expression does not occur in the Pentateuch, the prophetic books, or indeed anywhere in the Old

Testament.[14] Instead we find for violations of divine commands and ordinances the expressions "sin," "trespass," and "sacrilege," depending on the specific episode and the translator. All these terms clearly imply moral condemnation. But the element of divine condemnation appears to be more important than the moral aspect.

The situation becomes clearer if we look again at the word "moral." Throughout this study I have tried to use it in the same sense as the *mores* of William Graham Sumner. For Sumner both folkways and mores were a society's deeply ingrained popular modes of thinking and acting. They are forms of mass behavior. But mores differ from folkways in that mores carry a notion of social welfare. Thus a violation of one or more of its mores is a serious matter in any society. All sorts of sanctions will be brought to bear in a collective effort to punish a violation of mores. Such a violation is definitely an immoral act. A violation of folkways is much less serious, and generally results in nothing more serious than embarrassment. The person who violates folkways intermittently is treated as a clumsy oaf or an oddball, not a social menace.

With these considerations in mind, it becomes clear that most of the divine ordinances discussed above had little or nothing to do with ancient Hebrew popular morality as expressed in its folkways and mores. A few, such as the Ten Commandments, do look like divinely sanctioned and somewhat severe versions of patriarchal morality in a seminomadic society. But most of the divine commands and ordinances were attempts to establish new mores and to prevent the ancient Hebrews from accepting the mores of the peoples whom they had conquered and among whom they had settled. Ancient Hebrew religion was in large measure innovative and antitraditional. Hence an appeal to traditional morality in support of divine command would make no sense. Through divine ordinances the priests of the new sole God were trying to determine the character of the Hebrew community down to the pettiest details on a day-to-day basis. For that purpose dietary restrictions were useful and important.

Human beings could be made to avoid eating specified things without enormous difficulty. The results were also a matter of public knowledge in a small community. Dietary restrictions enabled the priests to demonstrate their authority over the Hebrew people and the people to demonstrate their distinctiveness from Canaanites, Philistines, *et id omne genus.*

Once we realize that most of the divine ordinances were issued *against* prevailing Hebrew custom, the issues of moral responsibility and guilt become clearer. Prohibitions on theft, murder, and adultery, which are to be found in a large majority of human societies, are highly probable and significant exceptions that did correspond with ancient Hebrew mores. If we knew more, we might find others. But it is reasonably clear that very many divine orders were innovations. Over and over again God appears as angry at the Hebrews for violations of the Covenant and specific divine injunctions. These violations show that some Hebrews believed in the ability of ordinary human beings to choose whether or not to obey. In this sense they did have a concept of moral responsibility.

Ethical responsibility, however, is a more accurate term. Moral responsibility refers to norms prevalent in the society. Ethical responsibility can refer to these but also refers to violations of transcendent standards. Still, there is a problem. The opportunity and ability to choose is plain enough in the case of dietary restrictions. But how about the case of a mildewed house?

To emphasize this distinction is, I suggest, to fall into the trap of anachronism by imposing modern forms of reasoning on the ancient Hebrews. For them, ethical behavior meant complete obedience to divine ordinances. Scale disease for humans and houses came from disobedience to God and was therefore an ethical fault. At this early stage when the priests were still struggling to establish monotheism, they ran the risk of overmoralizing human behavior. Everything from murder to eating pork became a moral failure, as monotheism was used to judge so many aspects of human existence. Furthermore, all moral failings took on roughly the same degree of emotional intensity. Even when the scripture reports a method of purification or atonement, terror forms a steady backdrop. And only a Moses can make a deal with God for leniency. Today the Hebrew universe looks like a terribly unlivable one, with pollution and death lurking behind every corner. I suspect that to many ordinary Hebrews at the time it looked the same way: "Such evil deeds could religion prompt," as Lucretius remarked about a half century before the beginning of our era.

In closing, it is appropriate to place the ancient Hebrews in a wider historical setting. They lived under a terroristic theocracy supported and justified by monotheism. The Hebrews, of course, did not invent monotheism. Their religious authorities forced it on them. Those who doubt this assertion would do well to read Isaiah and other prophets. The struggle to impose monotheism permeates the Old Testament, not just the Pentateuch. One cannot make the struggle disappear by labelling it as an essentially ancient myth only dimly related to human behavior, though mythical elements are clearly present. As a major part of the struggle, the advocates of monotheism took up widespread beliefs in pollution that had their threatening aspects, but were trivial in comparison with what happened after their absorption into monotheism.

Monotheism itself did not spring up out of nowhere. The belief in a supreme god ruling over minor deities long preceded monotheism. Nor was monotheism by any means the only legacy of Hebrew culture. The ideal of justice independent of social and economic status—that rich and poor alike should be punished for their crimes instead of the noble and well-to-do being legally entitled to milder penalties—is a major Hebrew theme. Once again it appears most clearly in Isaiah.

Finally, to paraphrase a famous English remark about democracy, Hebrew monotheism displayed no nonsense about monogamy or sex in general. The Song of Solomon is one of the loveliest examples of erotic literature in any culture. The huge number of Solomon's wives may well be legendary, but it is one of those legends that epitomizes the longings of a culture.

Despite all the exceptions and contrary trends just mentioned, the invention of monotheism by ancient Hebrew religious authorities was a cruel, world-shaking event. It had to be cruel in the general sense that any group identity is liable to be formed in hostile competition with other groups. It was world-shaking in the sense that Christianity, despite the astonishing and dramatic tolerance of Jesus towards fallen women, took over ancient Hebrew vindictive intolerance, amplified it, and institutionalized it. In the eighteenth century, as we shall see, vindictive and persecuting intolerance became secularized. For the Western world, and only the Western world, we can discern a line of historical causation that begins with the monotheism of the ancient Hebrews; runs through the heresies of early Christianity, the slaughters of the Crusades, the Inquisition, and the Reformation; turns secular in the French Revolution; and culminates in what the great nineteenth-century Swiss historian Jacob Burckhardt presciently termed "the terrible simplifiers"—Nazism and Leninism-Stalinism. The long long route from the ancient Hebrews to Stalinism was a river of social causation fed by many different streams and dropping floating debris all along the way.

Yet despite all the twisting and turning and historical debris, the river has a clear identity and an obvious ending point (or way station?) in twentieth-century totalitarian regimes. Without this long line of causation providing a readily available model of vicious behavior, it is very hard to see how these regimes could have come about. The monotheistic tradition by this time was hardly the most important cause of Nazism and Stalinism. But it was, I suggest, an indispensable one.

It is, of course, out of the question to treat all aspects of the historical fate of monotheism in a single book. The next chapter shows monotheism's fate at a crucial point in French history. We shall see how gentle people can become bloodthirsty and how mass anger can, with religious sanction, kill large numbers of people—without resort to gas ovens and other technological attainments of the twentieth century.

Purity in the Religious Conflicts
of Sixteenth-Century France

LIKE THE preceding chapter on the Old Testament, this chapter concentrates on the role of purity-impurity in a specific society during a specific period of time. We will focus on the specific meaning of the words purity and impurity, and especially the behaviors connected with them. Rather than giving a general historical summary of this crucial phase of French history—the Wars of Religion, for example, are barely mentioned—this chapter makes exploratory soundings into certain aspects of this period, mainly crisis points, chosen on the basis of the familiar anthropological principle that cultural assumptions emerge most clearly in a time of severe conflict. That, of course, is the reason for choosing this period of French history in the first place.

From the standpoint of this inquiry negative findings are just as important as positive ones. We are as interested in the absence of a conception of purity, or a very weak emphasis thereon, as we are on historical periods that display a very strong emphasis (i.e., where it appears as a guiding principle over a wide range of behavior). Likewise we are especially interested in the different meanings given to conceptions of purity and pollution in different societies and even within the same society.

To understand these meanings, and especially to avoid the anachronistic imposition of our own notions about purity and pollution, it is necessary to provide rather full information about the social and historical contexts in which they occur. The same procedure is necessary in those instances where there is no record of any mention of purity or pollution, despite circumstances that lead one to expect their occurrence. Without an awareness of context, misinterpretation is highly likely.

A few words about the sources may be helpful here. The preceding chapter on the ancient Hebrews as revealed through the Old Testament drew almost entirely on primary sources, that is, the available written records closest to the events under consideration. From one respectable point of view it would be desirable to analyze the conflict between Catholics and Huguenots mainly on the basis of primary sources such as speeches, letters, and sermons. Limitations on the availability of such primary materials and on the time it would take to analyze them make their exclusive use a counsel of perfection. Nor would that really be so desirable. The emphasis in this inquiry is on the public meaning of purity and its social influence and sources. Thus a letter by an obscure Huguenot provincial nobleman discussing at considerable length the notions of purity and pollution would have a certain piquant interest yet very little relevance for this investigation.

At the same time it would be rather odd to make no use of some printed primary sources. Two sources have been the object of close reading and interpretation. One is a collection of sixteenth-century Huguenot anti-Catholic songs that provides valuable glimpses of popular stereotypes. The other, at the opposite end of some bumpy continuum between popular thinking and professional philosophy-theology, is Calvin's three-volume *L'Institution Chrétienne*. This book is to Calvinism what *Das Kapital* is to Marxism. I have studied Calvin's major work more than once for other purposes. For the present chapter I have devoted a whole section to Calvin's conceptions of purity and sin.

Purity and the Creation of a New Religious Identity

The first stirrings of religious reform in the French Catholic Church about which we have any record put in their appearances in the early 1520s. They were attempts to "purify" the system of worship by putting an end to the practice of making money by selling religious services. There was also marked uneasiness about the cult of the saints, which, it was claimed in France and elsewhere, had become a superstition usurping the worship of God alone. At this beginning stage the reformers looked forward to a peaceful transformation, by educational means, of religious doctrines and practice.[1]

In this early phase, too, reform was chiefly an affair of the elite. Between 1530 and 1538 the main source of recruitment for reform was the leadership of the French Catholic Church. It attracted bishops, intellectual leaders, and men of affairs, especially diplomats. The guardians of official doctrine evidently understood the need for reform. Hence church leaders served as patrons and protectors of Reform intellectuals. In a good many elite circles of the day there was a thirst for faith and certainty amid the confusion of the times. This emotional thirst contributed to the acceptance and spread of early movements for reform.[2] Then the object of reform was still the restoration of the original church, not the promotion of a new dogma. Nevertheless, according to Imbart de la Tour, still a highly respected scholar, these early efforts at restoration produced enough of a psychological shock to prepare the way for heresy.[3]

Imbart de la Tour's classic account of the early stages of the Huguenot movement, then called simply "the Reform," which we have followed up to this point, stresses its elite character. Was there not also an indigenous, spontaneous movement somewhere near or at the bottom of the French social pyramid? That kind of question is always difficult to answer, because such movements may surface briefly in a remote locality then disappear without leaving any trace in the historical record.

In the case of the Huguenots there appears to have been plenty of religious discontent, mainly in the form of anticlericalism, and mainly among the poorer artisans in the towns, where it could combine with economic protest and give a shiver to the better sort in the towns. The conditions for a large-scale religious upheaval appear to have been present. Yet the upheaval was no more spontaneous among the masses than it was among the elite. "Outside agitators" were necessary to set people in motion in both cases. The absence of an indigenous and spontaneous French Protestantism is not all that surprising as soon as one reflects about it. As anthropologists emphasize, it is much easier to borrow ideas than to invent them. Applying this principle, we notice rather rapidly that the content of Calvinism is mainly a heated denial of Catholic doctrine and practice.

This denial came rather easily and appears to have been prominent in the early phase of the Reform. There were other non-polemical, or even antipolemical traits in the early phase, but they disappeared as the movement grew and spread, thereby secreting its opposition. The famous nineteenth-century French historian Jules Michelet, whose multivolume histories gave him space to explore in detail as well as to vent his spleen against other historians, gives an account of how the popular and plebeian reform began. For this account Michelet draws on a report by the famous scientist Bernard Palissy, who died in the Bastille in 1589 or 1590, shortly after his arrest as a Huguenot. Michelet's tale seems somewhat idealized. Nevertheless it is at the very least a charter myth.

One poor but literate artisan, says Michelet, would explain the meaning of the Bible to another who could not read. The explanation met a psychological need and the practice spread widely. The effect was that gambling, banquets, violence, and scandalous verbal expression disappeared. Law cases diminished, city dwellers no longer went to play in inns. Instead they withdrew to their families.

In the beginning the Reform had no ministers and no precise dogma. It was reduced to a sort of moral revival, a "resurrection of the heart." Its adherents believed themselves engaged in a simple return to primitive Christianity—in those days a potentially explosive act, more so than its adherents realized.[4] Their return to a "pure" version of Christianity remained a central tenet of Huguenot beliefs about themselves for at least the era of the Wars of Religion (1562–1598), and probably much longer. It was the key to their new identity.

For a long time after the beginning, believers in the Reform had no notion of resistance. Their respect for authority was unbelievable and extended even to the point of their own death at the hands of authority. Michelet reports several moving examples. They disapproved highly of the peasant revolutionaries active in Swabia in 1525 and also of the Anabaptists in Münster in 1535. For the followers of the Reform in France their ethical principle was "Who takes up arms is not Christian." Catholics, on the other hand, displayed no indecision in taking up the sword. The Reform's martyrs showed themselves intrepid by confessing their faith in the face of death.[5] One example of martyrdom reveals the current glorification of marriage. A married Augustin, about to be executed, was told that he would be pardoned if he called his wife a concubine. He refused and died for her. As Michelet put it, he left his legitimate wife a widow with a martyr's glory.[6] This moral firmness in the face of death was a source of wonder and amazement on the part of Catholic spectators. The favorable impression it created could have encouraged the spread of Protestantism.

According to one dependable source, the early recruits to the Reform were indeed mainly little folk. This situation lasted until about 1550. With the accession of King Henry II (1547–1559), Calvin's prestige and other causes produced a sharp change. The legal profession, merchants, and noblemen began to swell the ranks. Most important of all was the adhesion of several great nobles of the realm around 1558. They included Antoine de Bourbon, the king of Navarre; Prince de Condé; and Admiral Coligny. With this infusion of new elements, especially the highest aristocracy, the pacifist submission to persecuting authority came to an end.[7]

We may now turn to a series of recent local studies to learn what the Huguenot movement and Catholicism meant in the lives of ordinary people in different parts of France.

A study of popular religion in the province of Champagne during the sixteenth century demonstrated what services Catholicism and the Huguenot faith performed for their adherents. The study, though confined to Champagne, sheds much light on issues dividing France. Both religions put a heavy emphasis on what they could and would do for the individual after death, and only secondarily what they could do to assist people in the crises of their life. On this earthly aspect the Catholics apparently had a somewhat more attractive offering. For both, nevertheless, the effect on how one was expected to live one's life depended heavily on promises and threats about the life to come.

In Champagne, as elsewhere in western Europe, what the Catholic clergy provided and what the local well-to-do wanted were continuing prayers for the dead, in large part to shorten their stay and diminish their suffering in purgatory. In the words of the author of this study, "Catholicism at the end of the Middle Ages was in large part a cult of the living in service of the dead."[8] Saints played a crucial role. As long as they were treated with respect, they never punished. The excess merit they had acquired enabled them to intercede with God on behalf of ordinary mortals. This excess merit filled the treasury from which the pope drew indulgences.[9] Evidently, popular Catholicism was an easygoing religion that provided ways to defuse feelings of guilt that might otherwise have led to self-torture and mental breakdown. Yet it is important to recall that in practice the Catholic treatment for guilt long resembled capitalist medicine at its height in the United States. Guilt-control worked strictly on a fee-for-service basis: the more guilt, the bigger the fees and incidental expenses. By no means everyone could afford the fees.

The cost of religious services became a favorite target for Huguenot sarcasm. In this way the Huguenots tried to turn a major attraction of Catholicism, its easygoing stance toward sin, temptation, and impurity, into a severe liability. The frequency with which the Huguenots made these charges, especially in their popular songs (to be discussed shortly), suggests that the charges were effective.

Not every Catholic religious service to humanity was directed towards the afterlife. Different churches acquired their special relics for the cure of personal ills. There were miraculous cures and healing saints.[10] The Virgin Mary seems to have been the most widely loved and trusted figure in the Catholic religious hierarchy of those days. Presumably she could do many things in addition to using her gentle hand to guide the dead through purgatory to the ultimate goal.

Huguenot religious doctrine took shape against Catholicism. Groups very often create their own identity through opposition to other groups. Huguenot advocacy of purity in the sense of a return to the simple practices of Gospel Christianity implied and demanded paring away the subsequent Catholic accretions: the cult of Mary and the saints, the mass and other paid services and prayers for the dead, the magical presence of Christ in Holy Communion. Perhaps because the Gospels reported Christ as very active in curing the sick and raising the dead, the Huguenots apparently held their fire against these features of Catholicism.

What then did the Reform offer to put in the place of the Catholic services just sketched? At first glance Galpern's answer sounds approximately like "self-sacrifice and virtue." There is nothing astonishing in this answer. Under situations of unfamiliar social disorder and emotional and intellectual disarray, there is liable to be a substantial audience for dogmatic certainty and strict social discipline. St. Paul reacted in exactly this fashion shortly after the founding of Christianity. We have lived through similar experiences on a worldwide scale in the twentieth century, with new variants in sight already for the twenty-first.

In sixteenth-century France moral purity meant (1) scrapping the whole Catholic apparatus of forgiveness, (2) adopting strict controls over sexual drives and the pleasures of the bottle and the table (as the doctrine develops we hear much less about control of aggression, gentleness, and peacefulness), and (3) all this for the sake of creating theocratic utopia on earth *à la Genève*. Theocratic utopia was Calvin's idea. Apparently it was not part of popular hopes and musings.

Now that we have been able to discern the meaning of moral purity in this specific historical context, let us return to Champagne and ask what the Huguenots could offer to and demand from a potential convert. What, if anything, did Huguenot moral purity mean among the demands of daily life? The answer is very simple in general terms and rather complex in terms of concrete behavior. The convert had to withdraw from Catholic society and join the Huguenot social world.

A candidate for conversion was not expected to know much about religion—just enough to be negative about Catholicism. The convert was expected to reject the Catholic system of mutual aid among Christians. That could have been quite a wrench unless the convert was already quite negatively disposed towards it, as seems to have often been the case. The convert was to reject private masses, confraternities, and the pomp and circumstance of big funerals. In other words the convert had to renounce membership in the community and estate that depended on sharing in religious ritual for the benefit of all.

However, the convert was not to be socially isolated. The new Huguenot group's members defined themselves normatively as sharing in the revival of true religion. Their goal was the victory of religious reform, not a new society (except as a possible by-product). Ties among men were deemed less important than the renewal of the bond between man and God.[11]

Huguenots emphasized a direct approach to God. Hence they rejected all quasi-divine intercession. They had no use for the Virgin and none for the saints. Thus Reform hotheads mutilated statues, to the horror of the faithful. Huguenots were expected to be self-reliant and to develop self-esteem. Aware of his or her own sins, the Calvinist believed that God would accept a person as he or she was, justified by faith rather than social acts.[12] With its emphasis on predestination and God's utterly arbitrary way of choosing who would be saved or damned, Calvin's own views, to be discussed shortly, were a great deal more complicated and much less cheerful than ordinary Catholic opinions. Nevertheless, Calvin himself spoke of faith as a device for avoiding eternal damnation and gaining salvation. Thus it is quite likely that Huguenot self-confidence about sin represents the way dour Calvinism filtered down to a mass audience.

Two points are striking about this account of what Calvinism had to offer. The first is that most of the doctrine is negative, a severe critique of Catholicism. That was probably a help to the Huguenot cause. Shared hatreds are very effective in enabling people to get on with one another. The second point is the emphasis on self-control, especially in the form of a work ethic. The importance of a "strong work-ethic" type of personality for modernization in the West has been the subject of so much scholarly discussion that it would be out of place to do more than mention it here.

To summarize and review the creation of a French Protestant identity, the effort began in the 1530s with small, scattered groups professing a return to a pure and original form of Christianity. In this beginning stage these individuals were gentle, peaceable advocates of submission to authority, and against violence, yet willing to submit as martyrs to the Catholic authorities of the state. In 1536 an official and authoritarian doctrine appeared in the form of Jean Calvin's *L'Institution Chrétienne*. By 1559, twenty-three years later, there were enough of them to hold a national synod that adopted Calvinist doctrine and a Presbyterian form of church government. Around this time they also became known as Huguenots. From the very beginning they faced persecution, which of course stiffened their beliefs and gave them the sense they were a self-chosen opposition. Persecution remained continuous, if erratic, except in the territories temporarily under Huguenot control.

Thus by 1561, according to Galpern, France had a self-righteous Protestant minority enjoying momentary and limited toleration by the crown. Though still a minority, the original tiny and peaceable groups of believers had coalesced into an angry, threatening, and threatened multitude.[13]

THE CONCEPT OF PURITY IN CALVIN'S
L'INSTITUTION CHRÉTIENNE

Shortly after the publication of *L'Institution Chrétienne* in 1536, Calvin managed to acquire predominant influence in the Huguenot movement. Though Calvin was by no means a spontaneous product of indigenous French Protestant discontent, there is clear evidence that he resonated to their grievances, incorporating them in his learned theology. A Huguenot popular song, to be discussed shortly, dated four years before the publication of Calvin's most famous work, sounds very much like Calvinism before Calvin.

Calvin himself was a carefully trained intellectual who managed to take over the Huguenot movement through the force of his intellect, the strength of his personality, and his flair for political maneuvering. In these three crucial aspects he closely resembled Lenin. As in the case of Lenin, it is impossible to understand the victorious leader without some knowledge of the doctrines propounded by that leader. It would be presumptuous to attempt a new general interpretation of one of the most famous texts in Western history. Hence what follows is limited to the way moral purity appears in Calvin's major work.

In his major text Calvin devoted a great deal of attention to the concept of purity. He did so in very much the same way as the Old Testament. In both, purity had to do mainly with sex. Religiously approved sexual behavior was pure; so was virginity or complete continence, according to Calvin. A virtue not be scorned, virginity was not, he added, given to everyone. Since man was not created to live alone, and from the curse of sin was even more subject to the need for companionship, God, Calvin tells us, gave us the remedy of marriage for this need. Whence it follows, according to Calvin, that the company of man and woman outside marriage is accursed.[14] For Calvin, in this key passage "pure" is a strictly religious term, whose opposite is "accursed" (*maudite*): "God forbids lewdness. . . . He requires of us purity and chastity." Thus purity and chastity are synonymous.

These restrictions are derived from a specific conception of man. (Oddly enough, woman does not enter the discussion at this crucial point.) God created man with the power of free choice and moral responsibility.[15] Calvin insists on this point to make sure that we mortals do not blame God for Adam's faults and moral weakness.[16] Supposedly, Adam was pure in his original creation. But his moral fault created rotten offspring with hereditary contagion.[17] Here we have an explanation of human miseries that carefully avoids putting the responsibility on God. Instead, the causes are Adam's impure behavior with the apple and with Eve, though these mundane details are not spelled out in this polemical passage. Nevertheless, the meaning is clear enough: Adam's moral weaknesses are the cause of all the wickedness and suffering since his day.

Thus we have a definition of evil as a force of "accursed" behavior, or impurity, and an explanation of where the impurity came from. It was all Adam's fault, not God's. Was there anything living human beings could, according to Calvin, be expected to do in order to cope with this inherited tragedy?

Very little, though it seems to me that Calvin left more play in his determinist theology than is sometimes recognized. To be sure, Calvin has next to nothing to say about the pains and misfortunes of this life except to assert that men better put up with them, especially if they come from the actions of a tyrannical ruler. The only real hope is salvation in life after death, *if* one is lucky. By no means everyone can look forward to salvation, even if that person has led a life of chaste self-discipline and assiduous devotion to labor in the status assigned by God.[18] According to the theory of predestination, perhaps the most famous aspect of Calvin's doctrines, God, before creating the world, decided quite arbitrarily and for his "bon plaiser" who will be saved, who is without stain before his face. God's "bon plaiser" overrides all possible merits.[19] On the opposite side, God's judgment about who will be delivered to damnation is "occult and incomprehensible even though it be just and equitable." In the next few sentences Calvin partially retracts his thesis that God's judgments are not to be known. According to Calvin, God marks out the elect by calling them out and justifying them, while he deprives the others of knowledge of his word and the sanctification of the [holy] spirit.[20] Presumably, God informs the elect of their good fortune only after their death, whereas the others would be deprived of knowledge of God during their lifetime.

As just described, the system seems quite watertight, and for believers utterly terrifying. No amount of virtue and good works will serve to avoid perpetual damnation. This thesis was of course a blow against current Catholic practice, which by then had made salvation into a commodity in the Marxist sense of the term: something freely reproducible, which could be bought and sold in an open market. Calvin's system may or may not be ethically superior. But it certainly does not look like a set of beliefs that would encourage the simple "bourgeois" virtues that Calvin elsewhere advocated. Instead, it looks like a set of beliefs that would lead to despair and moral paralysis. It is more frightening by far than a banal "purity is its own reward—and do not count on any other."

In the light of these doctrines it is hardly surprising that Calvinists were by and large a gloomy lot. Yet they certainly did not suffer from moral paralysis. Quite the contrary! Why? What enabled them to escape from the trap of predestination? There is probably more than one answer to this question. A very important part of the answer, nevertheless, is that Calvin himself left an escape hatch for getting out of this trap.

The escape hatch was *faith*. God gave us an impossible task: to live according to the law. Failure means death and eternal damnation at the hand of God. The human situation is hopeless. Yet there is a way out: faith in the infinite mercy of Jesus Christ the Redeemer (N.B., *not* the saints, as in Catholicism. Once again Calvin engages in what economists call "product differentiation"). To paraphrase slightly, all mankind is impure. But faith in Jesus Christ will save those who have this faith. Hence faith brings salvation, purity.

It is legitimate to ask why Calvin chose faith as the agent of salvation instead of some moral virtue or a collection of such virtues. We, of course, have no evidence of what went on in Calvin's mind when he made that choice. On the other hand, by this time there was already abundant evidence about the importance of faith for religious and other types of human organizations. Faith, more specifically the "right kind" of faith, is what keeps an organization going. With strong-enough faith an organization can overcome severe obstacles, including its own defects, and remain active. Without faith (or as we might say today, with a loss of legitimacy and faith in its mission), even an organization with excellent resources will shrivel and die. Calvin, among all major religious leaders, was most keenly aware of the organizational imperatives facing his remarkable intellectual creation.

POLITICAL INVECTIVE: CATHOLIC IMAGES OF HUGUENOTS

In this section and the next I shall present publicly expressed Catholic images of the Huguenots and vice versa. Though these images changed over time in response to changing circumstances, a few themes stand out on account of their continuity.

The first major expression of Catholic official opinions on the religious divisions in France took place in the 1560–1561 meeting of the Estates General, the first one to be held since 1484. It took place at a time when there were high hopes of arranging a peaceful modus vivendi between Catholics and Huguenots, hopes soon to be disappointed.

The famous moderate chancellor Michel de l'Hôpital gave the opening speech in 1560, a remarkably candid one for a moderate in his position. Instead of playing down the religious differences or trying to paper them over, he at once singled out religious differences as the source of major discontents and sedition in the realm. But unlike zealous Catholics he refused to advocate the annihilation of dissidents. Instead, for Catholics he proposed a policy of moral improvement to undercut Huguenot accusations.

Towards the Huguenots he was much more severe. He began by asserting that for some perverse souls religion was nothing but a pretext for sedition, an opinion widely expressed later. About sedition Michel de l'Hôpital was merciless, despite his reputation for moderate compromise. "If there were a leper," he

39

asserted, "you would chase him from your city. There is all the more reason to chase out the seditious ones." At the very least, seditionists were impure, even to a distinguished moderate.[21] As might be expected, the orthodox Catholic attitude toward the Huguenots was even more hostile and placed more emphasis on them as a source of pollution. Moderates like Michel de l'Hôpital were willing to leave the Huguenots more or less alone so long as they refrained from violence and sedition. The orthodox Catholic position would have no part in this limited tolerance or in distinctions among different kinds of Huguenots. For Jean Quentin, speaking for the clergy at the royal session of the Estates General on January 1, 1561, it is evident that the only good Huguenot would be a dead Huguenot:

> We ask that the sectarians be forbidden to have any dealings with Catholics, that they be treated as enemies and that those who have left the kingdom because of their religion be prevented from returning. It is the prince's duty to use the sword he has received and to punish with death those who have let themselves be *infected by the mortal poison of heresy.*[22]

As official spokesman for the clergy on a very solemn occasion it is highly unlikely that Jean Quentin was expressing extreme opinions. It is far more likely that these views were widespread among the French clergy at that time. It was a short step from finding Huguenots to be polluting to cleansing the realm by rooting them out and destroying them. Michel de l'Hôpital did not take this step. Marie de Medici did attempt this a dozen years later, with only the haziest notions of what her actions meant. In due course it will be necessary to look more closely at this horrifying yet revealing crisis, the Massacre of St. Bartholomew.

Before proceeding further, it is necessary to explain in some detail the meaning of religiously inspired sedition in sixteenth-century France. It was a much more emotionally threatening crime than it is today in our mainly secular age. It was an attack on the king. Together with the Catholic Church, over which the French king had considerable control, the king was expected to produce a dependably regular and predictable social world based on law and order. In turn the social order was a mirror of the order in the universe, by which the sun rose and set at predictable times and the seasons followed one another in their expected sequence. The king, of course, never completely succeeded in imposing order. (In fact even a strong king like Louis XIV had to put up with disobedience and disorder to a degree that seems astonishing to some modern scholars as well as contemporary observers.) And the seasons could get out of kilter, sending frost when people expected warm sunshine. Yet the king was expected to try hard, and certainly succeeded enough of the time to make royalty appear socially necessary. Hence an outright attack on the king in the form of sedition was terrifying. If the source of dependability in the social world disappeared, what would happen next? The same worries surfaced when the king seemed manifestly weak, immoral, and incompetent, as was the case with the last Valois king, Henry III, who ruled 1574–1589, that is, during the most violent crisis in Catholic-Huguenot relations.[23] Sedition threatened to destroy what few certainties there were in daily life, to make the once firm ground underfoot roll and tumble as in an earthquake. This aspect helps to account for the very high emotional charge connected with religious controversy. Since sedition posed such a dangerous threat, it not only justified but required terrifying measures to eliminate or even just control it.

Shortly after the opening of the Estates General, where Michel de l'Hôpital on December 13, 1560, threatened severe measures against any seditionist moves from the Huguenots, there took place an even higher-level gathering of the French elite in another effort to resolve the religious dispute by diplomacy and reasoned argument. The occasion became known as the Colloque de Poissy. It was a general gathering, or synod, of the French National Church, called late in 1561 partly because the pope, unwilling to make concessions, was dragging his feet about calling further meetings of the Council of Trent. Synods were expected to provide an authoritative, all-Catholic response

41

to issues troubling France. In the absence of any papal blessing for their peacemaking, the French court put on its best pomp and circumstance for this meeting of the two religions: King Charles IX, accompanied by(1) his mother, Catherine de Medici, (2) the duke of Orleans, his brother, and (3) the king of Navarre (later the great French king Henry IV) and his queen, presided over the opening session as if it were a meeting of the Estates General.

For a time all went well. Theodore de Bèze, celebrated Calvinist writer and debater, spoke in the place of Calvin, who sent him there. Bèze outlined the doctrines of the Reform, showing where they agreed with the doctrine of Roman Catholicism and where they did not. According to a modern historian, "The clarity of his exposition, the gravity and precision of his choice of words and the chorus of his eloquence had contained the passion of his audience"[24] (an echo here of French pride in their language?). But when Bèze reached the issue of the Eucharist, he asserted that the body of Our Lord was as far away from the bread and wine as the highest sky is distant from the earth.

That remark torpedoed hopes for a reconciliation. An excited murmur spread through the audience. The cardinal de Tournon said to the king and queen, "Did you hear this blasphemy?" Catherine de Medici at that moment saw no agreement was possible. A week later (September 16, 1561) the court reassembled for what looks like an anticlimax, a speech by the very traditional cardinal de Lorraine presenting traditional themes about ecclesiastical authority and the Eucharist.[25]

Thus, in addition to being suspected of sedition, the Huguenots were accused of blasphemy uttered at the highest level of their own organization. Either accusation was enough to rule a person out of human society. In late-twentieth-century language, they became dehumanized and demonized.

As if that were not enough, there were other damning traits. Especially for the poorer Catholics in Paris, the visible Huguenots were rich. They were also obviously members of the ruling inner circle: for example, Coligny, Condé, Henry of Navarre. There was, of course, a sharp contradiction between being members of the establishment and being seditious blasphemers. For a short time this was just one of the painful contradictions people tolerate for the sake of living in human society. But in sixteenth-century France the tension became too severe. Who was to be a member of the establishment and who was to be defined as a seditious blasphemer were issues over which men killed one another in the inconclusive Wars of Religion (1562–1598). The human carriers of two conceptions of purity and impurity, after futile attempts at reconciliation, found themselves in mortal combat, without either side being able to defeat, far less destroy, the enemy.

Thus a crucial aspect of the Wars of Religion was the near absence of the notion of legitimate opposition, either in practice or theory. In sixteenth-century Europe this concept was well over the historical horizon, concealed behind the kindly veil that hides the future's horrors as well as its blessings. On the face of the matter, compromise and legitimate opposition are just about impossible anyway in a religious conflict, because deviance from an orthodox religious belief is a very serious evil, a threat to the whole social order. The deviant individual is either damned or polluted, or both. The only way out of this dilemma is to diminish somewhat the supremacy of a religious view of the world, to give some recognition to other values such as peace, order, prosperity, the welfare of the political community, and the state. The weakness of a system of compromise and legitimate opposition was not for lack of trying along these lines. Marie de Medici's complete lack of a sense of religious commitment was an essential part of the early Catholic leadership's attempt at accommodation. But Bèze's position on the Eucharist posed an impossible condition. That attempt to legitimate evil was an outright failure. Later on, as the conflict began to seem hopeless as well as destructive, the *Politiques* had somewhat better luck by emphasizing secular values.[26] The most famous Politique, Michel de Montaigne, put his finger on the central issue of religious conflict in his observation that "it is setting a high value on one's opinions to roast men on account of them."[27]

43

POLITICAL INVECTIVE: HUGUENOT IMAGES
OF CATHOLICISM

The main Huguenot complaints about French Catholics were plain and simple. For a Huguenot a Catholic was, if an ecclesiastical officer, part of a corrupt and exploitative organization. The Catholic Church supposedly charged excessive fees for services such as private masses. Again, the church had acquired huge amounts of property, especially landed property, by illicit means. Despite this wealth it continued to extract payment from the poor in the form of tithe. On this score Huguenot grievances fused with general popular complaints, in a way that contributed very noticeably to support for the Huguenots among the poorer segments of the urban populations.[28]

The Calvinists, a term that can be used interchangeably with Huguenots soon after 1536, also accused the Catholic Church of falsifying Christian doctrine for the sake of justifying its wealth. This the church supposedly did by deemphasizing early Christian doctrines and replacing them with its own commentaries and "unbroken" tradition of exegises that went back to St. Peter. At a more personal level Catholics were charged with being given to fornication and adultery. The charge seems to have been leveled especially at clerics who broke the vow of chastity. But it was by no means limited to them. Instead, it was part of a general attack on the lack of instinctive restraints and "inappropriate" delight in the pleasures of the bed and the bottle that apparently marked both late medieval and early bourgeois civilization. Finally, after the Massacre of St. Bartholomew in 1572, Catholic officials were widely and correctly accused of mass murder.

Looking over this list of accusations and complaints, one is struck by the almost total lack of complaints about ordinary Catholic citizens. The only negative feature about them may have been that their sexual morals could "stand work" (as ship's carpenters used to say about a vessel whose soundness they suspected). All the rest of the accusations are directed against clerical officials. Thus the grounds for conflict appear relatively narrow if the mass of the population were to be left undisturbed. However, the masses had powerful reasons for fearing that they would not be allowed to live their own lives. Both Calvin's own doctrines and, even more significantly, the moral police he introduced in Geneva gave an ominous warning about what would happen under a Calvinism victorious.[29]

Up to this point our discussion of hostile images and styles of criticism and vituperation has drawn on major public statements by major public leaders, both Catholic and Huguenot. Their statements certainly reveal the main concerns on both sides. Otherwise we would have to believe that the leaders paid little or no attention to what their followers wanted to hear. Still, it would be worthwhile to learn how ordinary Catholics and Huguenots felt and expressed themselves on the literally burning issues of the day. Unfortunately I have not found any useful body of evidence for Catholics. But for Huguenots I have come upon a revealing collection of songs, satirical and otherwise.[30]

Most, perhaps all, of these songs reproduce standard anticlerical themes and abuses. As such, anticlericalism antedates the Huguenots by several centuries.[31] Evidently the Huguenots drew their popular doctrines from this ancient treasury. They had little need to work up a new ideology on their own.

What then was the content of these snatches of musical vituperation?

Song 1 (1532, or four years before the appearance of Calvin's *L'Institution Chrétienne*), presents a very full list of the targets of Huguenot moral indignation. They include ignorance, errors, idolatry (here equated with prayers to any deity except Jesus for redemption from sin), the host in Catholic religious ritual, the Antichrist that consumes everything, thieves with their bulls and pardons, the "stinking" mass ("be content with one redeemer because every other man is a liar"), clerical orders, monks, nuns, hermits, false prophets, idle bellies, and lewdness.

Here the entire ritual apparatus of Roman Catholicism is the object of moral indignation and contempt, both expressed at a

45

rather high voltage. By itself this little song, presumably at the very least a rough sample of popular Huguenot sentiments, reveals how little possibility existed at that time for a modus vivendi between the two religions. It is also a convincing demonstration that Calvin knew and articulated popular grievances, even while he damped their fire with a theological cloak.

Song 1 presents the main themes of popular Huguenot doctrine, or, better, what Huguenots refused to believe (Note that Huguenot popular doctrine is heavily dependent on Catholicism in the sense that it is almost entirely a negation of Catholicism). Therefore the discussion of other songs can be limited to themes not found in Song 1, or merely adumbrated there. There are thirty-one satirical songs in this part of the collection.

Song 3 (1546) is supposedly the plaintive song of a Protestant preacher who has hoped for a long time that one day he would enjoy the power and the freedom to preach the Gospel in France. He is made to sound bitter and discouraged: "If no one wants to receive it [the Gospel], God the eternal will take vengeance." In this little fantasy, disappointment leads to destructive aggression.

Song 5, dated before 1555, is a platitudinous ditty exhorting the three estates to serve God "in pure truth." It reveals the superficiality of popular political thinking as well as its religious context. God's grace effaces the sins of the perfect true believer. (The saving power of faith apparently had become an article of popular religion.) Then come the complaints and exhortations. Men of the church sell sacraments. (It appears that some Huguenots believed religious services should be free goods for consumers.) The nobility should observe the law and control their appetites. Workers on the land and good merchants should avoid doing evil, and should not be covetous or do anything shameful. There is no mention of any concrete or specific actions in these general exhortations, though they indicate a general awareness of current political and economic issues.

Song 11, dated before 1555, asserts that the pope and his agents are a bunch of rascals and wolves: Give them some ringing coins and they will save you. Bordier suppressed two verses in this song, one on the nuns, because they were "trop libre."

Song 13, verse 8, dated 1532, expresses at this early date a strong willingness to resort to violence: "If truth cannot win by right and by scripture, by pen and ink, burn, drown, kill in abundance." Catholics must have been aware of this murderous current in Huguenot thinking. The reverse must have been true as well. On this account too there is no mystery about the failure of attempts at reconciliation. Despite the reports of Huguenot opposition to violence in the beginning days of their movement, the struggle against the Catholics rapidly became a matter of life and death. In fact it was more serious because it concerned what happened to people after death.

The rest are rather ordinary anticlerical miscellanies: Song 14, verse 10, dated before 1555, has a hostile remark about church officers living off fornication; Song 15, verse 3, some lines about priests who sleep with nuns. According to Song 16, verse 8, in the mass the priest claims to pardon everybody's sins and thereby gives joy to trespass. By and large the songs make sin and Catholic treatment thereof seem quite enjoyable. This envious and dour note in Huguenot doctrine could have been quite attractive to an audience looking for security and self-discipline. That, of course, is a central aspect of moral purity.

In the songs I cannot recall even a phrase about the horrors of hell and the terrors of damnation. Perhaps these negative aspects of Calvinism were not so prominent in popular consciousness. From the experience of other cultures as well as our own, one would expect these themes to be prominent mainly among the old, the sick, the disappointed, and the easily frightened. Could "official" Calvinism have drawn disproportionately on such sources? Or was the gloomy side of Calvinism mainly a literary echo of the Old Testament?

The absence of any explicit expressions about purity versus pollution is from the point of view of this inquiry even more striking. If there were some remarks about purity, they must have been so minor as to escape notice. Evidently, popular Calvinism made little explicit use of this pattern of thought after the 1536 appearance of Calvin's magnum opus. On the other hand, an implicit distinction between pure and impure remained basic to the whole Calvinist position. The Catholic commercialization of access to salvation was impure. Purge Christianity of this dross, including saints, masses, and indulgences, the Calvinists claimed, and what remained would be pure, i.e., some form of primitive Christianity.

CRISES: FROM RELIGIOUS CONFLICT TO CLASS WAR?

The religious cleavage in French sixteenth-century society was mainly, though not entirely, a vertical cleavage, with both rich and poor on both sides of the religious divide. There was also a cleavage, at times a very sharp one, between rich and well-to-do on one side and the poor on the other. In many places and over the long haul religious differences exacerbated the conflict between rich and poor. Henry Heller, in a most illuminating monograph (cited in note 28), has shown how urban artisans suffered from the economic depression of the times, how the Huguenot heresy appealed to them and encouraged them to revolt, with little if any success, against the town elites. Fortunately for these elites Calvin's insistence on obedience to unjust authority—for Calvin there could be no other—helped greatly to damp down these urban uprisings.

What Heller describes appears to have been a normal situation that included occasional outbursts of violence, one also where religious differences defined much of normal conduct. There were also at least two major occasions where the religious conflicts erupted into class slaughter. For a brief moment during the slaughter religious affiliation largely ceased to matter. What did matter is that the elites in both cases not only made slaughter legitimate for their own "good" reasons but demanded and encouraged it. In the Massacre of St. Bartholomew's Day (August 24, 1572), those who did the killing were mainly the

Paris poor. Their victims were well-to-do Huguenots, or in a good many cases just plain well-to-do. The other main example was what became known as the Carnival in Romans, a town near Grenoble on the right bank of Isère just before it flows into the Rhône. There the town elite carried out a preemptive killing of the poorer elements in the town, who had shown some signs of a possible uprising. We shall look closely at these two critical outbreaks.

The background of the St. Bartholomew Massacre was this. By the time of the last Valois king the tensions and contradictions in French high politics had reached a point where assassination appeared to be the only effective way to change political leaders and policies. Meanwhile the chief of the Huguenot party, Admiral Coligny, seemed to the powerful Queen Mother, Catherine de Medici, and other major French leaders to be pursuing on account of his Protestant beliefs and connections a policy potentially very dangerous for the French monarchy and France itself: Coligny wanted France to give military help to the Protestant rebels in the Netherlands. This was part of a plan to create a large and powerful Protestant bloc in northwestern Europe.

Though Catherine de Medici had in the past given much support to Coligny, she veered away from what looked like a very risky future for her son, the king. Her politics were generally in terms of personalities, more specifically the personalities of the members of her family. For that matter Coligny had given evidence that he was not altogether trustworthy on that score. Five years before, in 1567, he had joined an abortive Huguenot plot to march on Paris and capture the king.[32] Catherine now decided to have Coligny murdered on the occasion of a huge festival in Paris celebrating the marriage of the flower of the Huguenots, Henry of Navarre, later to become king of France as Henry IV. The attempted assassination failed. Coligny was badly wounded but alive, only to be brutally murdered shortly afterwards.

No source that I have seen ever hints that Catherine and her son, King Charles IX, decided to kill two birds with one stone: authorize the murder of the wounded Coligny *and* a general massacre of the Huguenot elite, conveniently collected in Paris for the great wedding. But that is exactly what happened.

Between them Catherine and the king gave their royal blessing to the massacre. Charles IX is reported to have announced, "Kill them all," thus making mass murder legitimate.[33] The citizens of Paris, especially the disreputable segment of the poor, responded with glee, grabbing "suspects" and hacking them to bits with any means available. Except for being authorized and legitimate, the massacre was utterly spontaneous. Small groups without any overall coordination and no connection with one another did the killing. In that sense this collective murder was premodern. A work of mere manual labor, without twentieth-century social organization and technology for mass slaughter, the Massacre of St. Bartholomew still managed to destroy several thousand lives.

With killing made legitimate, the killers broadened their targets. Many Catholics were killed as well as Huguenots. To a great extent the massacre became a form of class warfare instead of religious warfare. Yet it was more than that. The general legitimation of murder allowed it to take place within the lower orders, though in these cases it seems to have been given a religious cover. Those against whom someone bore a grudge or who were a barrier to an inheritance were speedily dubbed Huguenots and slain.[34]

To elaborate a bit further on this grisly yet very significant evidence, the authorization of aggression did not release a huge flood of religious hatred. Instead, religion served mainly as a cover for other forms of hatred. When murder became a legitimate possibility, being poor seems to have been a more powerful influence on what one would do than being a Catholic or a Huguenot. The plebeian murderers in Paris were mainly Catholics. The rebellious poor artisans in the towns studied by Henry Heller were largely Huguenot.

Nevertheless, class slaughter is not a complete explanation. The authorization and encouragement of murder enabled *all* forms of murderous hostility latent in the population of Paris in

1572 to surface—to move from fantasy to reality. Children were among the victims, but also among the killers.[35] In this massacre ordinary human viciousness at its worst came to the surface, not for the first time and certainly not for the last.

Those responsible for the Massacre showed no signs of remorse. Instead there was relief at the apparent foiling of a dangerous threat. The people of Paris proclaimed Catherine de Medici "mother of the kingdom and preserver of the name Christian." The pope, among several forms of celebrating the Massacre, had a medal struck in honor of this "great day" and sent a cardinal to deliver it to Charles IX with his congratulations. Catherine de Medici is described as being so unable to comprehend religious hatred and so bound up in her petty personal intrigues that she could not suspect that anyone might be reluctant to deal with her after such a crime.[36] Queen Elizabeth of England, a Protestant facing her own religious divisions, did write a tart note to Catherine de Medici: "I don't care much about the admiral and his fellows. I am only astonished that the King of France would want to change the Decalogue so that homicide is no longer a sin." To this Catherine replies that if Elizabeth is unhappy about her killing some Protestants, she permits Elizabeth in revenge to butcher all the Catholics.[37]

Along with this cynical, barbed banter between two famous queens, in other quarters there were outpourings of moral condemnation and moral justifications of the slaughter. Catholics argued that the Massacre was designed to crush a Huguenot "conspiracy" arising out of a "Theodore Bèzian infection."[38] The expression "infection" suggests a way of thinking organized around the notions of purity and pollution. A paper by the well-known historian Natalie Zemon Davis provides abundant evidence in support of this interpretation. She studied religious riots, including the Massacre of St. Bartholomew, in sixteenth-century France. According to her findings a frequent goal of the religious riot was ridding the community of dreadful pollution. The word "pollution," she reports, was often on the lips of the violent in a riot. It sums up the dangers rioters saw in a dangerous and diabolical enemy.

Both Catholics and Protestants accused their opponents of uncleanness and profanation of holy objects. Both sides accused their opponents of illicit sexual behavior.[39] Especially in the crisis of a religious riot, polemical themes of impurity came to the surface on both sides.

For Catholic zealots the extermination of heretical "vermin" promised restoration of unity to the body social and the guarantee of its traditional boundaries.[40] Here pollution appears as an especially malignant threat to the cosmic order. So long as the rioters maintained a given religious commitment, they rarely displayed shame or guilt for violence. In other words, crowds acting out their beliefs about purity and pollution believed their actions to be legitimate.[41]

The Massacre of St. Bartholomew decapitated the Huguenot movement, killed many of its loyal followers, and put an end to whatever hopes the Huguenots may have had about conquering France. In that sense the Massacre was a major historical event. That is not true of the slaughter that ended the Mardi Gras Carnival in Romans on February 16, 1580. Though, as Le Roy Ladurie points out,[42] the Carnival was the climax of a vast regional revolt, its significance was purely regional. Nevertheless, and like the Massacre of St. Bartholomew, the Carnival reveals how the conflict between rich and poor could cut through the alignment between Catholics and Huguenots. Thus for our present purpose the significance of the Carnival in Romans lies in its resemblances to and differences from the Massacre of St. Bartholomew.

In both cases there was a severe threat to control by established elites from discontented elements in the lower orders. The conflict in Romans was between an upper crust of combined merchant-landowners and bourgeois patricians opposed to small-property owners in the middle ranges of common craftsmen.[43]

The "really" poor, numbering 1,300 to 1,500 in the town's population of 7,000 to 7,500, took part sporadically in street demonstrations. But they had no part in the leadership of the revolt organized by craftsmen and small-property owners. In addition to these forces of disorder were the agricultural laborers (called plowmen). Quite a number of the plowmen lived in the town.[44]

The central issues of the day were taxes and, behind taxes, authority and social prestige. By the time of the opening of the Estates General of the province of Dauphiné on April 19, 1579, tempers were close to the boiling point, despite or perhaps because of the unreasonably cold weather. Tax exemptions were a major reason for rising tempers. Nobles did not want to lose their exemption from taxes, and especially they did not want to pay taxes on land recently bought from commoners. Many nobles in the area had only recently acquired noble status and done so in order to escape the complicated tax burden of membership in the third estate. They were in no mood to give up their new privileges and dug in their heels to defend them. On the other hand, the commoners were angry because noble purchases took land off the tax rolls. Therefore the commoners faced an increasing burden on a shrinking tax basis.

Commoners at the same time were far from united. Le Roy Ladurie distinguishes three groups within the Third Estate: urban oligarchies (conservative and corrupt as he shows elsewhere), urban working men, and peasants already out of control, looting and burning. After a fashion radical craftsmen and peasants cooperated. In contrast, the rift between the urban elite and the workmen was rapidly widening, despite their mutual dislike of tax exemptions for the clergy and nobility.

Tensions over these issues had been increasing for some time before their climax on Mardi Gras, February 16, 1580. The town of Romans by this time was an urban islet in a sea of peasant revolts. The peasant war was fully under way by late 1578 and early 1579.[45] By 1580 the patricians in Romans felt hemmed in by hostile commoners in its working-class quarters and hostile peasants in the rural parishes.[46] What could happen if the two joined forces and overran the town? During and before the Carnival there was a good deal of strutting about by the sides in classic folk fashion, with not-so-veiled symbolic threats. In the course of this symbolic maneuvering, the town notables, either by design or by accident, managed to carry out a preemptive strike against the leaders of a possible urban revolt.[47] The coup succeeded and put an end to any prospect of revolt. There were only twenty to thirty deaths, including those executed for participating in the alleged plot for an uprising.[48]

However, the successful coup was not the end of the affair, at least not quite. The peasant revolt, though sharing some grievances with discontented townsmen, was independent of urban events. It continued for a short time after the bloody preemptive strike, but soon suffered a crippling defeat at the hands of royal military force. On March 26, 1580, the royal forces killed about half of a troop of some two thousand demoralized peasants. Even this massacre did not put an end to their uprising. They retreated to a fort, where they were reinforced by an elite cadre of Huguenot soldiers. (Inactive in Romans itself, Huguenots did their best to stir up the peasants.) On account of the Huguenot presence, royal forces at first refrained from attacking the fort. In September 1580 they did attack and take it. The fall of this fort marked the end of the peasant war in Dauphiné.[49] Thus the forces of order—as usual an historically specific form of order whose injustices will not bear too-close examination—won decisive victories on both the urban and rural fronts by means of force skillfully applied.

Let us now glance back at the Massacre of St. Bartholomew to see if the resemblances and differences between it and the Carnival in Romans crises reveal anything significant for the issues examined in this study. Both events, I suggest, show that when elite authority and controls were for any reason slackened, or as in the case of the Massacre of St. Bartholomew even temporarily suspended, a conflict between rich and poor emerged from the shadows. Taken along with Henry Heller's abundant evidence for artisans' economic grievances, these two crises indicate that a large part of the urban population were in a mood to fight about economic grievances, social discrimination, and the unfairness of the legal and political system. These, of course, became the fighting issues of the late-eighteenth century, not the late-sixteenth. Hence one cannot push this observation too far.

The conflict between rich and poor is, after all, as old as Western civilization itself. As we have seen, it was familiar to the ancient Hebrews, and of course the Greeks and Romans in classical times. In France of the late-sixteenth century the key elements of class conflict, something more complex than a simple struggle between rich and poor, still lay concealed over the historical horizon. There was no set of competing doctrines based on class alignments. Religion still governed social thought. Nor on the part of the poor was there yet any degree of organization directed towards gaining control of significant political levers in the society as a whole. What did exist was clear determination on the part of elites in both Calvinist and Catholic areas to prevent turbulent elements in the population from winning any share in power and authority.

The degree of cruelty was very different in the two cities. In Paris the elite released and encouraged popular brutality with horrible results. The Massacre of St. Bartholomew amounted to a blood purge, and a very effective one at that. In Romans there was no corresponding blood purge, merely a decapitation of the potential rebellion. The slaughter of the peasants shortly afterwards was not a blood purge or a taking of vengeance. The one thousand deaths were the result of military defeat in a pitched battle. In both cases, on the other hand, the elites got what they wanted from the degree of violence they released.

In urban France as a whole, as pointed out above, the violence and slaughter were justified on both sides in terms of religious pollution. For many Catholics the Huguenots were a disease or a polluting vermin that threatened to destroy the whole social order. For the Huguenots the entire Catholic ritual, with its belief in the real presence of Christ in the Mass, the veneration of relics, the cult of the Virgin, etc., formed a poisonous pollution of the true faith, to be rooted out by any possible means. As Natalie Zemon Davis has pointed out, commitment to the belief they were attacking pollution generally prevented any expressions of guilt or remorse by those on either side engaged in murderous slaughter.

Purity and Pollution in the Old Testament
and the Wars of Religion

By way of an afterword it may be instructive to ask what changes, if any, took place in the social implications of pollution and purity during the roughly two thousand years that separate the ancient Hebrews from the sixteenth-century French. The answer seems to be: astonishingly little. First, however, it is necessary to look more closely at the facts.

The surrounding circumstances were very different in the two cases. The ancient Hebrews during the formative period of their doctrines—from the Mosaic era up through the age of the prophets—were a group of not-too-impressive conqueror-settlers that formed a monotheistic island in a generally hostile, polytheistic sea. Hebrew religious authorities had to struggle continuously, and by no means always successfully, to maintain Hebrew religious and moral identity against the threats and temptations of this surrounding sea. Their conceptions of purity, impurity, and pollution arose out of this struggle. French Catholics, on the other hand, were not an island attempting to maintain their identity in the midst of a sea of idolatrous nations. Instead, the Catholics found themselves accused of idolatry by a mass of self-righteous purists who were not foreigners, but who, through copying foreigners, had sprouted wildly in their midst.

This difference in circumstances between Hebrews and sixteenth-century French does not appear to have had notable consequences. Rather, it is the similarities that had such dire results. In both cases there were leaders and followers who felt threatened in their religious, moral, and social identity by unbelievers who challenged the whole basis of this identity. In France the response to this challenge took some time to develop because at first the Protestant challenge seemed peaceful and trivial. That turned out to be a comforting illusion. Influential elements among both Catholics and Protestants were spoiling for total religious victory. Like the ancient Hebrews, both reacted by developing a vindictive, persecuting, and destructive sense of their own "pure" morality.

In terms of its effect on human suffering, the most significant of all these developments is the whole process of creating moral approval for cruelty. To create this moral approval it is necessary to define the polluting enemy as nonhuman or inhuman, that is, outside the range of human beings to whom one owes the slightest obligation as fellow creatures. Beyond that, the polluting enemy has to be defined as a demonic threat to the existing social order. Dehumanization and demonization serve to diminish or, in many cases, completely eliminate remorse or guilt at the most barbarous and sickening cruelties.

In the Old Testament we frequently come upon passages where this process occurs. Yet in any specific case it is hard to determine whether the passage represents advocacy of such measures by religious authorities or a reliable description of what actually happened. The most one can assert with confidence is that the ancient Hebrews were quite familiar with the threat of pollution and cruel ways of meeting this threat. In sixteenth-century France we know it was part of actual behavior. It could generate such ghastly actions as dropping babies from windows, stripping other corpses, and throwing them into the Seine.[50] Such behavior, frequent though it was in sixteenth-century France, occurred only in the white heat of passion during the religious riot. Nevertheless, there were other more organized forms of cruelty, such as the burning of heretics and the tortures used by both sides, that would have to be included in any assessment of horrors and miseries of this age. On balance this regularized and routinized cruelty may have been the most important contribution to human suffering.

This morally approved infliction of death with cruelty is a continuity that surfaced again in Europe in the middle of the twentieth century, a further reason for stressing its importance. The Holocaust was no outburst of white-hot anger. It was a highly controlled and organized affair, even though there were plenty of hitches, as in any huge, rapidly organized bureaucracy. As

Daniel Goldhagen has shown so vividly and with abundant evidence, there was the same dehumanization and demonization of the polluting enemy (in this case the Jews), the same lack of guilt and remorse. In many cases the executioners treated their grisly task like a summer outing, complete with snapshots, girlfriends, picnics, and the like—and the same kinds of superfluous cruelty. The French rioters in 1572 in outbursts of rage dropped babies from windows. German soldiers in 1942 shot babies in cold blood.[51]

Purity as a Revolutionary Concept
in the French Revolution

Bᴇᴄᴀᴜsᴇ the politically significant features in the concept
of purity—the dehumanization and demonization of persons
deemed impure—have come to light in preceding chapters,
this chapter and the next will give less detail about the social
background of the concepts of purity and impurity. The present chapter, the last on a Western society, will attempt to bring
out new elements in the Western tradition produced by a major revolutionary situation, as well as significant continuities
with the past.

Cʜᴀɴɢᴇs ɪɴ ᴛʜᴇ Usᴀɢᴇ ᴏꜰ Puʀɪᴛʏ sɪɴᴄᴇ ᴛʜᴇ Fʀᴇɴᴄʜ
Wᴀʀs ᴏꜰ Rᴇʟɪɢɪᴏɴ

In comparing eighteenth-century usage with that of the sixteenth century, one notices a sharp decline in the sexual connotations of purity. Purity has now become essentially a secular
term, often no more than a rather general indicator of appro-
bation. Its religious origin has all but vanished also. According
to a major scholarly dictionary, the first substantive use of *pur*
occurs in Montesquieu in 1721. Later, after 1792, it spread
widely during the Revolution to denote a person entirely given
over to a cause, a doctrine.[1] Unfortunately this dictionary gives
no specific reference to any text by Montesquieu, and leafing
through his major works I failed to come upon any remarks that
would support this claim.

Nevertheless, there is an essay by Rousseau that shows the notion of purity to be common intellectual coin by the middle of

the eighteenth century. The essay has a piquant flavor today as a criticism of the natural sciences and the consumer society long before either had achieved dominating influence on Western thought. In the title, Rousseau puts moral purity solidly in the center of his discussion: "Whether the Reestablishment of the Science and Arts Has Contributed to the Purification of Morals."[2] As might be anticipated, Rousseau's answer is an earnest, discontented negative. This discourse is in the tradition of the Noble Savage (the expression comes from Dryden) or more generally of the use of a utopian past as a stick to belabor an allegedly immoral and unpleasant present. This intellectual posture remains prominent at the end of the twentieth century and flourished intermittently centuries before Rousseau.[3] The savage is both noble and pure, that is, uncontaminated by the tastes and habits of civilization. Actually, in this essay Rousseau has very little to say about human beings in a state of nature and purity. His mind is set on attacking impurity, which he does indiscriminately with an air of youthful dismay. He takes aim at the vile and deceptive uniformity, the demands of politeness and usage that come from an overrefined taste and an art of pleasing reduced to principles (204–205). Our souls are corrupted in the measure which our sciences and arts have advanced toward perfection (206). He rings the changes on luxury, voluptuousness, treachery, and assassination. Sparta is praised; Athens condemned (207–211). Toward the close of the first part of the *Discours* there is a sentence that sums up its entire message: "There is the way dissolution and slavery have at all times been the punishment for the conceited efforts we have made to get out of the happy ignorance where the wisdom of eternity has placed us" (213). Here already, decades before the Revolution, purity has acquired populist traits: equality (the subject of another famous work by Rousseau) with a strong dose of asceticism, or at least hostility to luxury, and hostility to any form of science and learning that lacks a promise to improve and moralize human society. Such was the pure and simple society for which thousands were to be sent to the guillotine. For this, Rousseau's share of responsibility was minimal.

Others advocated similar ideas whose consequences were well over the visible historical horizon.[4]

Though Rousseau lamented the loss of purity due to the advance of civilization, the word purity was hardly on everyone's lips before the Revolution, and even after it was well started. For educated Frenchmen then, *pureté* was no word to conjure with. It was not, like freedom, equality, or their opposites feudalism and aristocracy, an expression that supposedly could unlock intellectual puzzles and release desirable emotions. The word does not occur among the numerous topical headings in Mornet's *Origines intellectuelles*. Nor could I find it in recent detailed studies of the Gironde, the first group with some claim to include Revolutionary intellectuals.[5] Its absence from such interpretations of intellectual discussion does not of course mean that the concept of purity was unknown or even unfamiliar. It was part of the French intellectual repertoire across a wide intellectual spectrum, as we shall see in a moment. However, there are good reasons not to expect much of a trace of this notion among Girondins. What they stood for is still a matter of lively discussion among historians. At the very least, however, the Girondins were moderates. Now moderates are unlikely to find purity an attractive trait. They want some mixture in their political sauce. Reasons of temperament as well as political strategy lead them to try for widely based coalitions—with little or no success in a polarizing revolutionary situation. Though moderates may use the term occasionally about secondary matters, purity is a concept far more likely to appeal to educated yet doctrinaire radicals.

For an example of a moderate in revolutionary times we may glance at Brissot, certainly a very well known and equally voluble leader of the Girondins. In a substantial sample of his memoirs, eight chapters out of fifty-nine, a total text of 472 pages, I found only one rather trivial use of the word *pur*.[6] Brissot asked an obscure writer with a reputation for intellectual honesty, "How can you, whom I believe to be pure, contribute to such an infamous journal?" The reply was, "I want to purify the journal, make it useful in preventing the evils that prepare anarchy for us."[7] That is evidence, if evidence be needed, that the concept of moral purity was common intellectual coin, even if rarely drawn from France's cultural bank.

On the other hand, like many educated moderates, Brissot, even if he hardly ever used the word pure, judged the state of French society and culture by a standard of moral purity. He characterized the entire French elite of his day as corrupted. The common peoples' lives he regarded as debased and ignorant.[8] In fact, he considered practically the entire French population corrupt, debased, and ignorant.

One wonders, therefore, what segment of the population could be a vehicle for constructive social change from this point of view. Education, about which the Girondins were enthusiastic, was the long-term answer. For the immediate revolutionary present the critical, educated elite appeared by a process of elimination to be Brissot's and others' candidate for leading controlled, revolutionary change. So far as I am aware, no one in the Gironde explicitly stated this quasi-Leninist thesis. For that matter, as we shall see, the Gironde's radical opponents also were unable to answer the fatal question of how and where to find a social base for the Revolution. By Thermidor 1794 their bloody efforts were a failure. The leaders of the French Revolution were the first to pose this question, which neither the leaders of the Russian nor Chinese Revolutions were able to solve. For all three the issue of moral purity among leaders and led became a salient aspect of their bloody disputes.[9]

We may end this discussion of moderates and moral purity with a few brief remarks about Danton, the most controversial character in the Revolution.[10] A case can be made for the thesis that he was not even a moderate. His last speech before the Convention on March 27, 1793, ten days before he was executed on April 6, 1793, was a masterpiece of revolutionary oratory, requesting the death penalty for critics of the Revolution. No doubt he was a political chameleon, changing the tone of his splendid oratory to suit the political occasion. At one point he asserted that his enemies were putting it about that he was the actual author of Marat's tirades.[11] On the other hand it is reasonably clear that he did not want to see France torn apart by internal factional quarrels, which he saw correctly were the result of strains and privations imposed on the population by the revolutionary situation. (His solution was to make enemies of the people at home and abroad pay for the Revolution.)[12] His desire to avoid tearing France apart provides enough ground for considering him a moderate. He may well have feathered his own nest in the pursuit of this objective. In any case one would not expect such a man, widely regarded as the greatest orator of the Revolution, to talk much about moral purity. That, I suspect, he left entirely to others, with perhaps a touch of contempt.[13]

If we can take it as obvious that the notions of purity-impurity would be at least familiar to the highly educated adherents of the Gironde, it is rather more surprising to come upon this usage in Hébert, the self-appointed and deliberately vulgar spokesman of the sans-culottes. On this occasion, however, Hébert used the expression in its old, sexual sense. In an attack on royalty, Hébert even threw mud at the very popular king, Henri IV, saying, "Never did an honest woman approach this impure [man] without getting soiled."[14] Presumably Hébert was sure that the sans-culottes could understand what he was talking about. Whether he judged popular sentiment correctly is another matter. After the Valois kings and their minions, a strong, hearty, heterosexual ruler such as Henri IV might have been widely greeted with a sense of relief.

Purity and Revolutionary Radicalism: Hébert

Hébert has just been mentioned in the discussion about the notion of purity being by no means confined to educated moderates. In what follows we leave the moderates behind and proceed to the heart of this chapter, an analysis of the most prominent figures in the radical aspects of the Revolution. Marat was certainly one of these. As a doctor, he probably had a better education than Hébert. He had a better and richer mind, and is much more interesting to read. On the other hand, it is reasonably clear that Hébert for several years lived the life of a sans-culotte and knew what he was talking about.[15] For that reason he is more useful for the purpose at hand.

Hébert was a model guttersnipe. His *Père Duchesne* is almost entirely made up of savage political invective with the word *foutre* scattered through the sentences (much the way a similar expression, beginning with same letter, occurs as a meaningless intensive in present-day vulgar English). But in the very large sample of *Père Duchesne* contained in the biography by L. Jacob, I found only one sexual reference. It refers to gossip accusing Marie Antoinette of incest with her son.[16] In Hébert's discussion of the episode, however, there is no indication that this incestuous behavior was perceived as in any way impure in the sense of polluting and therefore dangerous to others. Quite possibly, some individuals who spread or heard the rumors felt that way. But there does not appear to have been any big uproar over that theme. As mentioned above, sex lost its prominence in feelings about purity and impurity during this period.

Scattered references to purity in the active sense of purity (*épurer*) do occur in *Père Duchesne*. According to Hébert, one can purify a significant symbolic object such as a cathedral of its stupidity.[17] One could also purify institutions such as the government, a revolutionary society, or even a large body of individuals. "Through intrigues traitors have succeeded in casting doubt on the purity of the patriots' intentions," reads part of a speech quoted in *Père Duchesne*. Evidently, patriots, a term then signifying a high degree of revolutionary commitment (not at all loyalty to France as such), were expected by radicals to have "pure intentions."[18]

Hébert at one time was elected to a commission charged to prepare a purification of the Jacobin society.[19] This episode, together with others just cited, reveals the revolutionary usage of "purify" to mean getting rid of people with insufficient revolutionary commitment. In itself this is no electrifying discovery, though it is sobering to see purity once more used as the justification for humanity's cruelest behavior. More striking in this context is the rather low salience of purity in what Hébert had to say. References to purity are few and far between. There is no mention of it at all in his thumbnail sketch of a free man.[20] Is the very limited reference to purity due merely to the fact that Hébert was deliberately writing a scurrilous sheet? Even if the answer turns out to be an only mildly qualified yes, it would be significant to a degree. The history of scurrility in Western civilization reveals much about that civilization. Before adopting this simple answer, it is necessary to look carefully at what he was scurrilous about. What and whom did he hate and why? How did he explain the pain and suffering of the sans-culottes? What part, if any, did notions of pollution play in this version of popular reasoning?

Human beings as individuals and members of a social group generally have a set of explanations and remedies for their misfortunes and disasters. Hébert and the sans-culottes for whom he claimed to speak are no exception. Theirs was a strictly secular diagnosis and remedy, a novel development limited mainly but not entirely to Western society in the eighteenth century. Previously and elsewhere both diagnosis and remedy had a strong religious component.

As befits a journalist, Hébert hammered out a set of themes identifying and castigating the enemies of the Revolution to explain why it was in such trouble. It was indeed in serious trouble, especially towards the end of Hébert's career and afterwards. The consequence of war and revolutionary confusion was a dramatic reduction in the food supply for Paris. In turn the shortages alienated more and more of the sans-culottes from the Revolution. By March 24, 1794, this dilemma led to the execution of Hébert and by July 27, 1794 (9 Thermidor), to the execution of the executioners, Robespierre and Saint-Just. Before and during this acute situation the radical revolutionaries generated a diagnosis and remedy for the obstacle to the Revolution. It took the form of revolutionary commonplaces, a

65

set of formulae or catalogue of enemies. The formulae could adapt rather easily to changes in the situation by, for example, adding new names to the list of those persons to be execrated and executed.

Hébert's diagnosis and remedy was very similar to the other revolutionary commonplaces and clichés circulating at that time, though somewhat more crude. As is usual in the case of such stereotypes, there was more than enough truth behind them to make them plausible. Treachery by high military and leaders appears as an extremely important, perhaps the most important, reason for the Revolution stalling and blundering.[21] Recent scholarship shows that corruption was indeed widespread.[22] The least plausible of these revolutionary commonplaces was to blame their troubles on the activities of foreign agents and spies from states hostile to the Revolution, as indeed all states of any political power were. England's prime minister William Pitt was the favorite radical stalking-horse. Just about any mishap and misfortune appeared explicable to revolutionary radicals as the work of Pitt's gold and his agents swarming all over France. It is true that Pitt did have many agents in revolutionary France and spent large amounts of the British taxpayers' money supporting their activities.[23] Whether these activities had the slightest effect on French revolutionary politics is, on the other hand, dubious.

Another revolutionary commonplace was the activity of speculators, whose behavior undermined the whole revolutionary edifice. For Hébert speculators were an object of special venom. Among other activities they bought up scarce grain at cheap prices and sold it to the hungry people of Paris at high prices, supposedly making enormous profits. In the speculators Hébert had suitable popular explanation for these developments, though he did not live to see their most acute stage. A victim of Robespierre's and Saint-Just's "implacable revolutionary justice," he went to the guillotine along with several other radical leaders on March 24, 1794. There is a tragic irony in this end. More than other radicals Hébert touted the guillotine as the cure for the Revolution's failure. In his case it is fair to say that the guillotine was the sole remedy for the Revolution's weaknesses as diagnosed in his version of the commonplaces just discussed. These commonplaces all share a strong moral component. Together they portray the Revolution as failing on account of the moral failures of easily identifiable individuals.

Though Hébert's explanation in terms of identifiable individuals and their moral failings may seem odd to us some two centuries later, there are reasons for holding that attributing political success or failure to moral qualities is a widespread and characteristic human trait, still with us today.[24] It plays an important role in Herodotus' explanation of historical events and, mixed with more general religious conceptions, permeates Greek tragedy. The belief in moral responsibility for great historical events and decisions is not altogether false. Whether the idea has ever acted as a brake on dangerous leaders is another matter. It becomes lethal on a mass scale when combined with a powerful emotional commitment to some general notion of human welfare that turns out to be unachievable in the specific historical context. In Hébert's case the goal was not so much overall human equality as minimal economic security and social respect for the small artisans, journeymen, small traders, itinerant peddlers, and the like who made up the sans-culottes. A second-tier revolutionary leader, whose name I can no longer recall, said that the point of the Revolution was to put culottes on the sans-culottes. Hébert's program sounds feasible enough now, two hundred years later. It was not feasible then. Hébert had no conception of the "objective" social and economic obstacles. All he could see were individuals without revolutionary commitment scrambling to feather their own nest. From this point of view the only cure for the problems of the Revolution would be a liberal application of the guillotine. Hébert never had the opportunity to put his application into practice. Robespierre and Saint-Just did, and to a great extent they shared a body of revolutionary commonplaces with Hébert.

CHAPTER 3

PURITY AND REVOLUTIONARY RADICALISM: ROBESPIERRE

Looking at Robespierre after Hébert, one gets the impression of
coming upon a giant after studying a lively pygmy. Hébert was a
chattering scold with hardly anything in the way of a social program for the Revolution to accomplish. Instead he had a conventional set of enemies. For all his faults Robespierre did have
a definite set of aims for the Revolution. He was also perfectly willing, perhaps even eager, to accept responsibility for the major decisions and politics needed to achieve this objective. His version
of the aims of the Revolution displayed prominent elements
of the intellectually fashionable romantic egalitarian utopia. He
had only a hazy idea about how to get there. Mainly it was by re-
lying on the revolutionary enthusiasm of "the people." By "the
people" he meant those people from any social sector who shared
his enthusiasm. Those who lacked this enthusiasm were auto-
matically enemies of the Revolution, traitors and paid agents of
enemy powers. Robespierre explained every shortcoming of the
Revolution by a conspiracy against it. On this crucial issue Robespierre was no better than Hébert. Except for occasional remarks
about the proper direction for the Revolution, his collected
speeches and parliamentary remarks to the National Convention
are mainly diatribes against alleged conspiracies.[24] Despite his
superiority to Hébert, the poverty of social and political insight
seems incredible for a major revolutionary leader. As just mentioned, he had one explanation for failure of his revolutionary
policies or opposition to them: treachery supported by England
and other powers hostile to the Revolution. He had but one
solution: the relentless use of the guillotine.

According to the distinguished and impartial scholar William
Doyle's *Oxford History of the French Revolution,* Robespierre on
several important occasions opposed resort to the guillotine.
Doyle asserts that especially after the defeat of the Vendéans,
Robespierre became "very conscious that needless excesses would
discredit the Revolution."[25] My impression is that Robespierre

68

was always contemptuous of foreign opinions hostile to punitive revolutionary actions. But let us look at the evidence Doyle adduces in support of his generalization. He cites Robespierre's attempt to save Marie Antoinette from the guillotine. However, David P. Jordan, in *The Revolutionary Career of Maximilien Robespierre*, mentions two specific occasions when Robespierre called for her head, and in a series of subsequent references to her Jordan makes no mention of any efforts by Robespierre to save her.[26] In the same passage about Marie Antoinette, Doyle also refers to Robespierre's supposed attempt to save the Girondins from execution. For me that is the oddest claim of all because Robespierre's venomous attitude toward them is so well known.[27]

I have not found anything in Robespierre's speeches and writings to support Doyle's claim that he was one of the leaders who wanted to let up on the terror after the defeat of the Vendéans (December 12, 1793). If anything, the opposite appears to be the case, since it was during this period that Robespierre delivered on February 5, 1794, his famous speech on revolutionary morality (utterly pure) and revolutionary government. But I did turn up one nugget of entertaining information useful to this inquiry. It concerns Robespierre's defense of Danton's morals. Robespierre had a way of defending an associate shortly before calling for his execution. The public part of this latter task he left to Saint-Just. Robespierre's public moral reputation as "incorruptible" was spotless to the point of being prissy. Danton was the exact opposite: not above feathering his own nest, he had got himself a very pretty and much younger wife, and on at least one occasion was obscenely contemptuous of revolutionary rhetoric. Yet Robespierre could say of him before the Jacobins, "There is no man whose domestic morals are more simple, more pure and consequently more republican." In the next sentence he speaks of Danton as a man "whose principles are to enjoy an air pure and free."[28] This public judgment of Danton may do little credit to Robespierre's perspicacity. On the other hand, it demonstrates the importance of purity to its most important radical revolutionary leader.

This curious blindness did not, however, extend to other people's policies. Of these Robespierre could be an astute critic, and early in his career he could be a first-rate practical politician, as evidenced by two episodes having to do with price control. The best-known example occurred at the beginning of December 1792, when food shortages in Paris had reached crisis proportions, causing severe unrest among the sans-culottes. There were riots in other parts of the country. On December 2, 1792, Robespierre before the Convention attacked the economic liberalism that had nothing but bayonets to feed the starving, and, in addition, he proclaimed the right of subsistence as basic to all other rights of man. He also had concrete proposals to alleviate the shortages, such as removing obstacles to the circulation of grains within France.[29] The other episode, though much less important, is significant for showing Robespierre's intervention in administrative detail, this time as a committed liberal. A representative on mission to the Oise on the day after the adoption of the Law of Suspects (September 18, 1793) suggested on the basis of his experience that anyone who sold goods of primary necessity at an exorbitant price should be considered a "suspect" from now on—frequently the first step toward the guillotine.[30] The representative made this suggestion because he had been very successful in squeezing out food for Paris when on mission, where representatives usually had wide discretion. This suggested legislation received a surprisingly cool reception in Paris. Several deputies felt the proposal was too vague. Robespierre joined them. While praising what the representative on mission had accomplished, he did not want to see such behavior generally sanctioned by law. It offered too many opportunities for bad administrators to make trouble for good citizens. "It is not severe principles or rigorous laws that we lack; it is their execution," said Robespierre in the course of his brief intervention.[31]

These occasional flashes of political insight and liberal decency did nothing to alter the general drift and pattern of Robespierre's policies. (For a diametrically opposite opinion by a very distinguished scholar, see Mathiez's *Études sur Robespierre,* cited above.) The shortages and sacrifices due to revolutionary confusion, corruption, war against foreign invaders (brought to a successful conclusion just before Robespierre's death), and the use of the guillotine on a mass scale eroded popular support for the Revolution. The size of "the people" declined until it began to seem that Robespierre was the only one left. By that point he had begun to threaten colleagues on the Committee of Public Safety, refusing to name them.[32] To save their own skins several members of the committee turned on him. That was the end. After an unsuccessful attempt at suicide he was guillotined along with eighty other Robespierrists, including Saint-Just, on July 29, 1794.[33]

What part did ideas about purity and impurity play in this extraordinary career? They were very important in his conception of the form of society the Revolution should strive to create, the ways to achieve this society (that is, political morality during and after the Revolution), and finally in the self-image of "the Incorruptible" that he put before the public. His moral purity and revolutionary intransigence, qualities likely to have appeal only in a period of intense excitement, appear to have been significant causes of his ascendancy. Yet the most important explanation of his rise and fall is the simple fact that he managed to have all his potential rivals and critics guillotined, with popular acclamation, one after the other: first, assorted moderates in the Girondins (executed October 31, 1793); second, the execution of Hébert and other radicals (March 24, 1794); third, execution of more moderates, or at least antiradicals, in the person of Danton, Camille Desmoulins and others (April 6, 1794). With the high points of this career in mind, we may now tease out in more detail the meaning of purity for Robespierre and what he intended to convey to his audiences with this concept.

In a speech on the principles of political morality that should guide the National Convention in the Republic's domestic administration, delivered before the Convention on February 17, 1794, Robespierre, still at a high point in his power, spoke about the kind of society he, and presumably some others, regarded as the goal for which they were fighting. The main point was the peaceful enjoyment of liberty and equality, the reign of eternal justice whose laws have been engraved not in stone but in the hearts of men. Other points are more specific, while remaining at a level of very high-altitude morality. Low and cruel passions were to be held in chains, benign and generous passions awakened by the laws. "We want," asserted Robespierre, "to substitute in our country morality for egoism, . . . scorn of vice for scorn of misfortune, . . . the charm of happiness for the boredom of voluptuousness."[34] In a nutshell the aim of this blood-drenched struggle was, for Robespierre at least, moral purity.

Earlier, on the occasion of discussing the death penalty for Louis XVI, Robespierre remarked to his audience of revolutionaries that, having lived under "despotism" long enough to take many oppressive aspects for granted, the "weakness of our morals, depravity of our spirits" made it very hard to recognize and respond to the "purity of principles . . . implied by the free government to which we dare aspire."[35] Thus a society organized around moral purity appears here as a goal for an unspecified future and attainable only after a moral and intellectual cleansing— not to mention bloodshed—that today we would call brainwashing. On this score the secular version of purity was as much another worldly goal as its religious variants in the Old Testament tradition and during the religious wars in France.

If the outcome of the Revolution was to be a much greater degree of social and political equality as part of moral purity, it would require great popular support. Robespierre recognized this connection, though the recognition was shot through with romantic idealism. According to Robespierre, "the people" was the carrier of revolutionary ideals: "The people is naturally upright *(droit)* and peaceable; it is always guided by a pure intent."[36] In a discussion of representative government on May 10, 1793, he emphasized that "the virtue and sovereignty of the people" was the best "preservative against the vices and despotism of the government."[37] In a long speech toward the end of his career on the moral principles that should guide the administration of the French Republic, from which we have already cited his goal for the Revolution, Robespierre went so far as to speak of the "purity of the bases" of the Revolution. Their pure and sublime character, he went on to say, was both a source of strength and weakness: strength because it was the source of revolutionary enthusiasm, weakness because it attracted the hostility of all the evil elements in the population.[38] Though he does not refer specifically to "the people" in this passage, his statement shows that the people is an exclusive political category, designating Robespierre's political supporters. Nonsupporters were by definition enemies of the Revolution.

While Robespierre placed purity as a major revolutionary goal, to be achieved through reliance on the people as the main repository of purity and other virtues, from time to time he spoke about purity in a more instrumental sense. He stressed the importance of pure elections, pure in the sense of free from corruption in choosing officials under a representative government.[39] In general, Robespierre was suspicious of nearly all government officials, definitely including his own. The higher the officials, the more they ought to be pure, that is, take account of the public interest instead of private ones. Robespierre urged that the supreme elected body in the Republic should keep an eye on *(surveiller)* and continually repress public officials— hardly a penetrating suggestion. Then he went on to claim that the character of popular government is to be confident about the people and severe towards itself.[40] Once again the people emerges as the indispensable revolutionary panacea. This was one of Robespierre's recurring notions, perhaps the silliest one. In the long speech on representative government delivered on May 10, 1973, he remarked that "the ills of society never come from the people but from the government. How could it be otherwise? The interest of the people is in the public good. The interest of the man in an official post is a private interest."[41] If the society to come out of the Revolution was one of moral purity and simple joys, what did Robespierre see as the obstacles to this revolutionary march? More specifically, did he regard the obstacles and individuals therewith associated as morally evil and therefore impure?

As has already become plain, Robespierre as a revolutionary leader had a simple, binary image of the social world. On one side were the enthusiastic supporters of the Revolution. These were the virtuous. *Vertu*, a word used by Robespierre more often than *pureté*, at that time had lost its connection with female chastity, instead meaning commitment to the Revolution. On the other side were the enemies of the Revolution, together with the noncommitted or lukewarm. These appeared likely to become enemies. Enemies of the Revolution, actual and potential, were of course morally reprehensible, proper fodder for the guillotine.

The litany of reprehensible moral traits appears as early as his "Exposition de mes Principes" (May 1792). There he refers to the war started up by Girondin leaders in the belief that French political principles would sweep aside Europe's current rulers (the first idealist hope to shatter against reality) as actually a source of French internal divisions, "fomented by intrigue and corruption, favored by ignorance, egoism and credulity."[42] Robespierre was a moralist but no moral crusader. For Robespierre political differences became moral differences and opponents moral outlaws—lepers and menaces all at once. This dynamic appeared also under Lenin, Stalin, and Mao. Robespierre merely gave it a good rolling start. Thus when urging the execution of Louis XVI (December 3, 1792), he castigated the revival of an aristocratic defense, with its poisonous pens and shamelessness *(impudeur)* surpassing that of previous defenders of royalty.[43] The inference is obvious: good revolutionaries should execute the king before such propaganda took hold. From this diatribe it appears obvious that Robespierre had rather limited faith in his own revolutionary cause. Within a few months he would start shoring it up with the guillotine.

Robespierre's most general statements about the tragedies of world history and the enemies of revolution occur in his speech of May 10, 1793, on representative government: "Ambition, force, and perfidy have been the legislators of the world." Despotism, by which he means royal absolutism, he continues, "has produced the corruption of morals." Corruption, an expression he uses frequently, is, of course, the opposite of purity. In this situation it refers to the one who sells his soul to the stronger in order to legitimate injustice and render tyranny divine. Then one has kings, priests, nobles, bourgeois, *canaille*, but no "people," no men.[44] The explanation of humanity's tragic fate is strictly in terms of moral failures. But he does offer a social explanation of the moral failure in terms of the repeated victory of the stronger and the unscrupulous that creates despotism.

At the conclusion of his famous speech on food shortages, December 2, 1792, he gave his explanation of the convulsions tearing states (actually just France) apart at that time. As might be anticipated, Robespierre saw the conflict as a strictly moral one, with all the good on one side and all the vice on the other side. The struggles are nothing other than "a battle of prejudices against principles, of egoism against the general interest, of the pride and passions of powerful men against the rights and against the needs of the weak."[45] On a few occasions he did express his theory of political evil with explicit reference to impurity. In his speech on the principles of revolutionary government (December 25, 1793) he observed, "The day it [revolutionary government] will fall into the impure or perfidious hands, liberty will be lost. Its name will be the pretext and excuse of the counterrevolution itself. Its energy will be that of a violent poison."[46]

This characteristic mixture of moral condemnation and a conspiracy theory of politics appears in its most salient form in Robespierre's two-hour final speech to the National Convention on 8 Thermidor (July 26, 1794).[47] Though the speech earned applause, the next day he was driven from power to face the guillotine shortly afterward. From the speech itself it is obvious that Robespierre felt cornered. He was afraid that the revolutionary government would now really fall into "impure and perfidious hands." From the standpoint of a revolutionary radical, that, of course, is exactly what happened. But there is no sign that Robespierre understood what was happening or why. Almost all of this long, rambling oration is an account of conspiracies against the Revolution and of how Robespierre and his allies had managed to unmask each one in succession and save the Revolution. For any failure or weakness in revolutionary policy there was only one explanation, conspiracy (= impurity), and one remedy, the guillotine (to root out and destroy the rot and impurity). Clearly such a policy has rapidly limiting returns, because executions do little to change policies and a great deal to spread fear and loathing. By the summer of 1794 the Revolution was in fact doing rather well. It had cleared France of foreign enemies and the economy had been showing signs of improvement since the autumn of 1793.[48]

The radical phase of the Revolution came to an end on 9 Thermidor (July 27, 1794). It did not come to an end on account of massive hostility to the radicals. Robespierre's government had already crushed such outbreaks in the Vendée, Lyons, and elsewhere. Instead, the radical impulse destroyed itself because it had no goal except moral purity and no way of getting there except the guillotine. When Robespierre finally showed signs of moving against his close associates they turned on him.

Before setting Robespierre aside, it is necessary to discuss briefly his use of the concept of purity in relation to other revolutionary commonplaces. Is there a pattern here? If so, does purity have a commanding or subordinate place in this pattern? It is important to make these issues explicit because in an inquiry such as the present one the investigator nearly always finds what he is looking for, a discovery that by itself may be worthless. We need to learn not only what notions of purity-impurity were current but also to acquire some sense of their importance in current thinking and political action. It is also useful to recall that negative findings, while somehow less exciting, can be just as important for an inquiry as positive ones.

Neither purity nor impurity were Robespierre's favorite items of revolutionary rhetoric. His favorite rallying cry was *vertu*. In a rousing attack on the Girondists on April 10, 1793, for instance, he cried out, "Oh, all powerful force of truth and vertu."[49] Earlier, in a speech of December 2, 1793, he made a brief remark about the society to come when he said, "Learn to taste the charms of equality and the delights of vertu."[50] As these examples indicate, the literal translation of vertu as virtue is inadequate. First, what it does not mean: for convinced revolutionary radicals the term, at least temporarily, had lost its sexual and religious connotations. As a revolutionary slogan it had nothing to do with female chastity. Instead it meant unalloyed commitment to the revolutionary cause. On that score the meaning of the noun "vertu" and the adjective "pure" were the same.

As for the religious aspect, a strongly anticlerical revolution was hardly likely to accept a religious authorization for its moral code. Instead, revolutionary radicals promoted the thesis that human beings were naturally moral and gentle but became immoral from living under "despotism"—especially its salon culture of flattery and intrigue. What emerges from these contradictory impulses concerning the kind of society one ought to want turns out to be a set of petit-bourgeois virtues without their familiar Christian certification. We can be quite sure that they had existed in French and artisan circles for some time. They are socially necessary, not to be sneered at by "enlightened" intellectuals, and include the virtues of hard work, sexual restraint, honesty, the repression of envy, truthfulness, and the acceptance of legitimate authority along with the right to resist injustice and oppression. With acceptable if not necessarily authorized evasions, this moral code is that of the bulk of the population in civilized societies. In the case of the French revolutionary radicals there is, in reaction against the prevailing aristocratic culture, more stress on an antiseptic moral purity and its allegedly innocent contentment.

For Robespierre, then, purity and vertu represent both proper revolutionary behavior and the kind of society expected to result from the Revolution. Their opposites constitute the obstacles to revolutionary objectives. Here purity becomes the more significant notion. Purity is a separating idea that implies the existence of impurity. Impurity takes the form, among others, of corruption, and corruption is a favorite negative term in Robespierre's vocabulary. What is impure is also repulsive and to be avoided. One should not have anything to do with an individual whose revolutionary purity is suspect. Indeed corruption and other forms of impurity, like rotten timbers in a ship, should be cut out and destroyed to preserve the sound parts of the structure. This destruction, actually of human lives, not mere wood, amounts to the ultimate separation of pure from impure. With appalling consistency, Robespierre the Incorruptible pursued this logic of moral purity to its only possible end: his own destruction and that of the revolution he led.

PURITY AND REVOLUTIONARY RADICALISM: SAINT-JUST

After a sustained examination of Robespierre's abundant texts, those by Louis-Antoine Saint-Just are a welcome change, and not only on account of their brevity. Towards the end of his career Robespierre became a paranoid utopian. Aspects of this development of course appeared earlier. It is highly likely that Saint-Just also shared this hope that the Revolution might bring about the age of love, comradeship, and equality.[51] But about life after the Revolution, Saint-Just had very little to say. In his famous report to the National Convention announcing the compelling need for a truly revolutionary government (October 10, 1793), all that Saint-Just had to say about future joys were these few, very typical words: "There is not the slightest hope for prosperity so long as the last enemy of liberty breathes."[52] Saint-Just was not one to concern himself about the future of the Revolution when it looked as though the Revolution could founder at any moment due to the incompetence, halfheartedness, and foot-dragging of those who were supposed to be running it. Unlike Robespierre, Saint-Just did not put all the blame for this state of affairs on the corrupting actions of aristocrats, though he did have plenty to say on this score from time to time. He saw that incompetents appointed incompetents to the point where whole branches of government could become paralyzed. About such situations he did not mince words, calling the heads of the French armies "imbeciles and rascals."[53]

Again unlike Robespierre, Saint-Just was no spider living a protected existence at the center of a political web. Instead he left Paris for extended periods to spend time as a powerful official from the center with the troubled French army of the Rhine. When Saint-Just first came upon this army, he found a demoralized and defeated collection of soldiers. Discipline was atrocious, mainly due to the lack of trust between officers and men. Many officers, to put it mildly, were unsympathetic to the Revolution, while much of the rank and file shared the populist anger of the sans-culottes. To complicate matters further, a large contingent of the soldiers were German-speaking, which drew them towards their German-speaking enemies.

With a combination of stick and carrot, and a remarkable intuitive feel for human relationships, Saint-Just, with the help of just one colleague, managed over the course of several months to turn this demoralized mass of soldiers into a most effective fighting force, with the dash and bravery associated with the best French military tradition.

Saint-Just used the stick primarily against the officers. His main measure was to force them to live with their men, sharing their discomforts and privations, thereby gaining the men's respect. Previously many officers after the day's "work" took off to enjoy the attractions of the town such as the theater and undoubtedly others. According to an anecdote that may not be true yet accurately reveals the situation, when Saint-Just had just arrived and was as yet unknown, an officer came up to him in the evening and asked his way to the theater. Saint-Just arrested him on the spot. He also used the stick for some purging of the command structure. He was not squeamish about using the guillotine, and once urged that even small violations of military rules should receive severe punishment in order to give the impression that the authorities had eyes that noticed everything. Nevertheless, under Saint-Just executions appear to have been rare.

The carrot aspect of his policies was on behalf of the rank-and-file soldiers and requires only a brief description. Using his authority and prestige Saint-Just managed to extract enough food supplies to provide his men with decent rations, and enough blankets and clothing to get them through the winter cold. Some supplies came from other armies judged to have less need for them. Others came from hard-pressed towns and rural areas. The whole process looks like holding a pistol to Peter's head so that he can pay Paul to do the job. For reasons mentioned earlier, nearly everything was scarce.

It is all the more remarkable, therefore, that Saint-Just could put together a force that drove the foreigners off French soil and in effect put an end to the threat from the continental part of the anti-French coalition. That was his most concrete contribution to the Revolution.[54]

But that was not his only one. Saint-Just was the incarnation of the revolutionary intransigence and determination for which Robespierre correctly became known. But it was Saint-Just, *not* Robespierre, whom the Committee of Public Safety chose to present the justification and character of a new revolutionary policy before the National Convention. This speech of October 10, 1793, mentioned at the beginning of this discussion, has earned Saint-Just the reputation of theorist of terror. That is correct, but quite inadequate. He had a great deal more to say than merely attempt a justification for the terror.

As a report in the name of the Committee of Public Safety, Saint-Just's speech was an official and favorable response to the threatening upsurge of sans-culotte radicalism on September 4–5, 1793. The sans-culottes demanded several radical measures, of which at least one became law with some slight effect: a ceiling on prices and wages. The uprising also led to political maneuvering about the membership and the precise degree of radicalism to be displayed by the Committee of Public Safety. More or less radically inclined leaders won out there too.[55]

Without overly misleading simplification one can paraphrase the Parisian-radical message to the Committee of Public Safety as "Get serious and give us a real revolution!" Saint-Just's response, directed at second-level revolutionary administrators and the general public rather than the sans-culottes, amounted to: "Get serious and *make* a real revolution! Otherwise we are lost." The speech opens with the laconic observation that sets the theme for the rest of the performance: "The laws are revolutionary; those who carry them out are not." Some remarks follow, intended to put iron in the soul of the revolutionaries. Saint-Just asserts that the Revolution is a bloody struggle between its supporters and its enemies with absolutely no possibility of reconciliation. At the same time he is obviously aware that a substantial segment of his audience in the Convention does not share this belief. Hence he says, "You have to punish not only the traitors, but the indifferents themselves. You have to punish whoever is passive in the Republic and doesn't do anything for it." A few sentences later he adds, "One must govern with iron those who cannot be governed with justice; one must oppress the tyrants."[56]

As we have seen, this split of humanity into good and evil is characteristic of those who think in terms of moral purity. Saint-Just's explicit rejection of any possible middle ground or refusal to take sides makes his position especially ominous. It justifies regarding him as the major theorist of revolutionary terror. Along with this intransigence there is a curious streak of anarchism: "A people has only one dangerous enemy: it is its government."[57]

Saint-Just did not stop with this dazzling display of revolutionary rhetoric and its ominous threats. He went on to present, in very concrete and specific terms spiced with caustic remarks, what he believed to be wrong with revolutionary policy and what should be done to correct the situation. There has already been occasion to mention his central theme of revolutionary laws that come to nothing on account of halfhearted and sometimes hostile administration. The plague of inflation and its social consequences, as well as bad side-effects from efforts to combat it, were also a major concern for Saint-Just. Taking one billion, eight hundred million francs out of circulation was a big help to the people, he asserted. Nevertheless, for reasons probably clear enough to his audience if not to a scholar writing two centuries later, the combined effect of inflation and price-setting was to double the value of property. Saint-Just wanted to extract a tribute from those who had become "opulent" in this way and to establish a tribunal to force those who had been handling the Republic's funds to account for their fortunes. If, on the other hand, the government continued to issue *assignats* and they remained in circulation, "The cultivator will abandon his plow because he will make more by working for the opulent man. You will have fixed the price for products, one will take away from you the arms that produce them. If products become scarcer, the rich will know well how to get them, and the famine can reach its peak."[58]

Saint-Just's speech amounted to a call for a revolutionary war-economy, though the term did not come into use until the last stages of World War I. Revolutionary government control with a strong punitive edge was the central feature in Saint-Just's proposals. For the proposals to work, as Saint-Just emphasized, there would have to be an atmosphere of high morale and faith in the Revolution.[59] From the standpoint of our inquiry the most important feature of this crucial and, for its day, unique piece of revolutionary exhortation is a negative one. So far as I can see, there is not a trace of any notion of impurity (or its opposite, purity) in this text. Of vituperation against the rich, the crooked, and the halfhearted there is an abundance. But they do not appear in this speech as a hidden source of pollution and corruption, as they do at times in Robespierre's speeches. Instead, their effect is a simple and direct form of damage to the cause of the Revolution. The evil is sinister yet plain enough to recognize for anyone able to face disagreeable facts.

Does this mean that notions of revolutionary purity played no part in Saint-Just's public image? Hardly. The day after Saint-Just's call for revolutionary discipline, he, Robespierre, and others in the Committee of Public Safety reported the recovery of Lyons by an army of the Republic, adding, "The traitors and rebels are cut to pieces. The standard of liberty flies from the walls and purifies them."[60] Since this was part of a longer message sent as an encouragement to the army of the North, we can be sure that the conception of purity used in this message made good sense to any sympathizer with the Revolution. Those against the Revolution, traitors and rebels, polluted their surroundings to the point where some simple symbol of purification, such as a flag, was welcome, perhaps necessary.

Saint-Just's use of the word purity was limited to occasions of intense revolutionary excitement and action such as the recovery of Lyons. With one minor exception, it does not occur in the state occasions for grand programmatic orations. There is no mention of purity in his speech "On the Constitution of France," given on April 24, 1793.[61] Immediately following his speech the *Complete Works* gives a seventeen-page draft constitution that may not have been delivered orally. Under the title there is the pregnant motto "One cannot govern innocently." In these detailed provisions for the structures of a new French government, part of an effort tacitly abandoned amid the crisis of 1793–1794, Saint-Just made no reference to purity. Somewhat surprisingly the same is true of his famous speech "For a Revolutionary Government" on October 10, 1793, which justified the terror and demanded a thorough purge of France's government and society.

An exception occurs earlier in his first effort at writing a constitution, "The Spirit of the Revolution and the Constitution," one of several efforts made by a series of deputies to the Estates General. (Saint-Just would have done well as a political scientist in an American university during the 1920s.) The section on civic morals contains a bland remark about pure relations and feelings in an ideal family, and some lines later a sentence about the origin of French civil law in Roman law, "the purest source there ever was."[62]

The first major public occasion on which Saint-Just used the notion of purity in the political sense of distinguishing "us" from "them" did not occur until July 8, 1793. He gave his only previous speech, in favor of executing Louis XVI, on November 13, 1792. Like all his speeches, that of July 8, 1793, was a reaction to a crisis in revolutionary policy involving the use of the guillotine.[63] In every case Saint-Just came down squarely on the side of executing the accused. He justified this act as the only way to protect the interests of the Revolution and the safety of the revolutionary Republic against the individual interests and alleged counterrevolutionary plots of the accused. The record shows plainly that Saint-Just was the point man chosen to defend the dirtiest and cruelest acts of the Revolution. The texts show that he performed these tasks with conviction and relish.

On this score the July 8, 1793, speech was typical. It justified the arrest of thirty-two members of the Convention, the principal deputies of the Gironde, on the grounds of seeking to put the son of Louis XVI on the throne and contributing to a situation of civil war in France.[64] The arrests themselves were forced on the Convention by a radical uprising in Paris.

The accusations were by no means wholly imaginary. Large areas of France were rebelling against the revolutionary rule of Paris. It was at this point that the French Revolution began to devour its leaders on a large scale. Saint-Just was not yet ready for a massive bloodbath, and recommended leniency for those arrested who had merely been misled. For those who had fled, and thereby revealed their guilt, he would on the other hand have no mercy whatever. At this point he said, in effect, that a conspiracy can be good for us revolutionaries because it preserves the pure while it expels the impure: "It is the fire of liberty that has purified us just as the boiling of metals drives out of the crucible the impure scum."[65]

The next three major speeches, though they have very little to say about purity, contain revealing statements about the closely related themes of revolutionary authority and terror. The first speech carries the title "Report on Persons Incarcerated," and Saint-Just delivered it before the National Convention on February 26, 1794 (or 8 Ventôse, Year II by the revolutionary calendar). Thus it came after the execution on October 31, 1793, of all twenty-one Girondists, to some of whom, "led astray mainly by ignorance," Saint-Just had promised lenience. It also preceded the execution of Hébert and other sans-culotte spokesmen on March 24, 1794, and foreshadowed the execution of Danton, Camille Desmoulins, and others on April 6, 1794. *Coup à gauche; coup à droite,* as these bloody episodes have long been known. But what was going on behind them? To what were the executions, and more particularly Saint-Just's major public statements, a response?

One can identify three major elements in this situation. First, especially but not only at this time, come the sans-culottes and their spokesmen. Whenever the supply of food dropped off, the sans-culottes were liable to riot, demand price controls (anathema to the bourgeois leaders of the Revolution) and, above all, terror. Generally, popular demand for terror came from the sans-culottes. It was their answer to every grievance. In response to a food shortage during the winter of 1793 their leaders turned against Robespierre and his followers. On February 22, 1794, Hébert denounced the Robespierrists as "Endormeurs," roughly, the ones trying to quiet down all the protests.[66]

Meanwhile, by about the end of 1793 a good many members of the Convention had become horrified and frightened by the extremes of terror that had occurred many times during the provincial uprisings. These came to an end with the defeat of that in Vendée in December 1793. That was the second element. Thus there was some reason for members of the Convention to hope that revolutionary radicalism had actually run its course. When Robespierre came out against the extremist radical attacks on churches and priests because he feared such tactics would convince nobody and alienate many from the Revolution, there were many sighs of relief in the Convention and among respectable Parisians generally. A decree by the Convention on December 6, 1793, put an end to dechristianization.[67] Danton emerged as a leader of this movement of opinion, whose members became known as the Indulgents. His policy seems to have been what it was before: mainly to get Frenchmen to stop their murderous mutual fighting and—less emphasized at this time—dump the costs of the Revolution on conquered foreigners.

With the Indulgents we reach the third element in the situation. Since this was still a very tense revolutionary situation, by no means all of the Indulgents displayed indulgent feelings. Camille Desmoulins, for example, viciously attacked Robespierre, his one-time friend.

To sum up, Robespierre's policies had run into severe opposition from the radical left outside the Convention and from a so-called moderate faction within the Convention, as well as creating a mixture of unreal and unfounded hopes for better days among others. The reaction of the Robespierrists was, as we have seen, to use the guillotine for the surgical removal of opposing factions. Saint-Just, freshly returned to Paris from the reorganization of the army on the Rhine, received the task of making the Robespierrist policy palatable to the Convention and the general public.

To return now to the content of the speeches, the one on February 26, 1794, "About the Persons Incarcerated," is almost entirely an argument for revolutionary rigor, including terror. But as will appear shortly, there are inconsistencies and hesitations in the exposition that presumably reflect uncertainties in the Committee of Public Safety.

Near the beginning Saint-Just asks rhetorically if a society must not make the greatest efforts to purify itself when interest and avarice are the secret resources of those who try to corrupt everything. Must it not do this if it wishes to survive? Then he adds ominously, "And those who wish to prevent it from purifying itself do they not wish to corrupt it? And those who wish to corrupt do they not wish to destroy it?"[68] The political implications of purity in a revolutionary situation could hardly be put in a more succinct form.

But there is more. After some discussion of the nature of a republic, with the usual classical allusion Saint-Just asserts, "What constitutes a Republic is the total destruction of whatever is opposed to it."[69] By such opposition Saint-Just of course meant competing political factions, a widespread negative judgment in eighteenth-century Europe and by no means confined to French Revolutionary leaders. However, the factions, according to Saint-Just, were the result of corrupt morals, a complaint that runs through all his speeches. By corrupt morals he meant an individualist pursuit of selfish pleasures such as sexual intrigues, luxurious food and housing, and the eager pursuit of money and position by intellectual means. Corrupt morals he contrasted with a conscious and willing acceptance of obligations to society together with contentment in hard work, sexual restraint, and the idealized set of what today might be called "family values." All this was pure. Except perhaps for the emphasis on social obligations, it is hard to discern anything in Saint-Just's distinction between pure and corrupt morals that would fail to receive enthusiastic endorsement from the most reactionary United States senator or leader of the Christian Right, as well as a large number of less controversial figures. Thus the most radical and "pure" goals of the French Revolution became in two centuries the mental baggage of Western reactionaries.

One ostensible purpose of terror, according to revolutionary theory—Saint-Just did not speak for himself, but pounded on themes he knew would resonate with a revolutionary audience—was to destroy corruption and thereby enable virtue to flourish. Toward the close of this speech he made some intriguing remarks about terror. They contain in quite condensed form an explanation of its purpose, a warning about its possible misuse, and a hope for its disappearance that turned out to be mistaken. Justice, which is distinct from terror even if it often requires terror, "condemns officials to probity; justice makes the people happy, and consolidates the new order of things." Then comes the warning "Terror is a two-edged weapon, of which one serves to avenge the people, and the other to serve tyranny." Coming from Saint-Just that is a remarkably prescient statement. A third and most mistaken remark is to the effect that revolutionary terror, unlike that under tyranny, is but of the moment: "Terror has passed like a thunderstorm."[70] Probably the purpose of this last remark was to reassure Convention members who felt there had been enough terror. Indeed the whole speech is rather obviously an effort to convince doubters (1) about the necessity and morality of terror, and (2) that it would not last. It is unlikely that any revolutionary leaders who listened to the report realized that the worst of the terror was still to come.

The report ended with a decree recommended by both committees in the form of two articles. The first was a rather minor concession to the Moderates and Indulgents. It granted the Committee of General Security the power to liberate "patriots," the term for committed revolutionaries. But every individual claiming liberation would have to give an account of his or her conduct since May 1, 1789. The second article reaffirmed the sacred and inviolable property rights of patriots. In contrast, the properties of those known to be enemies of the Revolution were to be sequestered for the benefit of the Republic. A sop to the radicals, this measure was more likely to appeal to the peasants than to the turbulent Parisian mob, then the main source of anxiety.[71]

The next speech, "On Foreign Factions," given on March 13, 1794,[72] was the Committee of Public Safety's public reaction to the very real threat of a sans-culotte uprising provoked and led by Hébert and others. One would never know this from the text itself, which does not identify its leftist target by name. Instead, the speech is a fine piece of revolutionary rhetoric. After a few flourishes about the need for courage to speak unpleasant truths, Saint-Just announced to "the people" that it was "time for everybody to return to morality and the aristocracy to terror." Next he proclaimed the existence of a conspiracy set up by foreigners whose aim was a coup that would return France to a royal government.[73]

The speech is full of complaints about moral corruption, especially the taste for luxury, with which the foreign enemy hopes to destroy the Revolution. At one point Saint-Just does direct a shaft against indulgence (i.e., Danton and his followers) and goes on to claim that the faction of the foreigner (i.e., Hébert and the sans-culottes) and the faction of Indulgents work together at undermining the Revolution. This corruption and taste for luxury Saint-Just contrasts with the "comfort of moderation" *(aisance de la médiocrité)*.[74] In a later passage, which seems very much from the heart, he contrasts the frivolity of the aristocracy and its hangers-on with French society's acute need for productive work.[75] The most important contrast, however, even if it is for the most part implicit, remains that between the morally pure and committed patriot with "the fire of an ardent and pure heart," and the impure enemies of the Revolution, here "the impure remains of the royalists and rebels of the Vendée."[76]

Thousands of copies of this speech were promptly distributed in Paris. Arrests occurred the next day. The Committee of Public Safety ordered the public prosecutor to secure a conviction at all costs. On March 24, 1794, or eleven days after Saint-Just's speech, the guillotine took the lives of Hébert together with an assortment—twenty individuals had been arrested—of leftist leaders involved in what Saint-Just called a conspiracy to restore a royal government in France.[77] How many Parisians believed the accusation that the sans-culottes wanted to restore the French monarchy? Did Saint-Just believe it? We can never know the answer to these questions. Yet we know enough about the situation to suggest plausible answers that shed light on the way revolutions work themselves out. As for the rank-and-file sans-culottes, they were angry enough about their situation and hostile enough towards leaders in general to welcome *any* candidates for the guillotine, no matter who they were. As for Saint-Just and other members of the Committee of Public Safety, they could have suspected that if lack of respect for the revolutionary leadership went much further, the consequence would be widespread, tumultuous disorder, out of which could arise a new leader, a *chef.* That would be the real victory of the counterrevolution. In Saint-Just's speech there is much revolutionary fulmination against disorder, immorality, and lack of discipline, about which we can be sure the members of the Committee of Public Safety were seriously concerned as a threat to their own existence. In general, revolutionaries who have just come to power are especially acute to signs of public disorder.

After the speech that sent Hébert and the alleged leftist-royalist radicals to the guillotine, thereby supposedly purifying France of the malady of factionalism,[78] Saint-Just's next one was to do the same for Danton and the Indulgents.[79] The speech, however, seems rather an anticlimax. We have heard most of the rhetoric before, and through repetition it carries less conviction rather than more. In my opinion these reservations hold even though there are good grounds for concluding that the attack on Danton et al. was the most important speech in Saint-Just's career. After all, Danton was a much bigger fish than Hébert or any of his associates. He was also a great orator and a member of the Convention, where Saint-Just, against the advice of his committee colleagues, not so wisely insisted on confronting him publicly. Danton replied with such booming oratory that it attracted crowds in the street outside. The authorities had to whisk him off to jail to preserve their own version of revolutionary theater.

The first mention of the word "purity" occurs near the beginning of the speech, in a way that indicates that the idea hovered in the background of speaker and audience's thinking and played an important role in organizing the accusations, even though it was hardly mentioned again. "Conspiracies," said Saint-Just, "instruct governments to keep an eye on morals and to conserve the purity of the principles on which legislation rests." They are a sign, he went on, that one has neglected to correct many abuses, especially to punish injustice. Furthermore, the insensitivity of the laws to misfortune *(malheur)* and legitimate discontents has swelled factions (a bow to the dead radicals?), just as indulgence for the wicked or the corruption of officials has discouraged people's hearts and made them indifferent to the fatherland (a clear enough threat to the Dantonistes).[80] Thus the concept of purity formed the background for the burning issues and accusations of the day.

After this opening, the term itself almost disappears from the speech. It occurs only once in a vitriolic passage against one

Lacroux, a man "with an impure soul" and supposedly well known as a conspirator for a long time past. Actually he was not well-enough known to deserve an entry in the very full index of Monar's *Saint-Just* or Doyle's *French Revolution*. From the rest of Saint-Just's diatribe it seems that he was a general who intermittently tried to put a stick in the wheels of revolutionary progress.[81] More significant than the identity of this relatively obscure individual is the rarity of "impure" as an epithet of personal abuse in the public statements of both Robespierre and Saint-Just. Especially in the case of Saint-Just it seems as though impure was too general an expression to evoke the punitive response he wanted. Hence he used a mixture of concrete facts, alleged facts, innuendo, and suggestions of conspiracy, treachery, and personal dishonesty to bring about the condemnation of the victims. Despite the secular aims of the Revolution, failure to display the prescribed enthusiasm for them could be a "sin" with consequences as deadly as the wrong religious beliefs during the Wars of Religion.

These two trials, ending with the bloody public spectacle of serial execution, amounted to rituals of purification. "After having abolished factions," Saint-Just called out towards the end of his speech, "give to this Republic gentle morals." He continued: "Return to a society of mutual esteem and individual respect. Be in peace with one another. Have you not spouses to cherish and children to raise? Be well behaved and spread justice without seeking renown."[82] In other words, after passing through the ritual of purification may you live happily ever after in a world of pure morals, domestic bliss, and all-around moderation. As we have known for some time, things did not turn out that way. So far they never have, with or without a revolution.

Nine days after the execution of Danton, Camille Desmoulins, and the others, Saint-Just was awarded on April 15, 1794, the task of answering publicly on behalf of the Committee of Public Safety and General Security the question that must have been on many minds, "What next?" He chose or was asked to discuss five topics: police, justice, commerce, legislation, and crimes of factions.[83] His opening remark was ominous: "It is not enough, citizens, to have destroyed the factions; it is still necessary to repair the damage they have done to the fatherland." The remark sounded as though there was more purification to come, as was indeed the case.

Saint-Just was coming around to the opinion that if the Revolution were to succeed, it would have to create a new type of human being, one with a new set of emotions favoring the public good instead of personal and private advantages. In the meantime tighter administrative controls, including a good dose of terror, would be required to elicit the behavior necessary to keep the revolutionary society running and approaching its goals. Saint-Just appears to have been the first to have recognized the need to create more awareness of public needs. It is an issue to which the Communist leaders of the twentieth century, Lenin, Stalin, and Mao, devoted so much attention with so little effect.

Early on in his speech of April 15, 1794, Saint-Just presents an idealized model of what a revolutionary ought to be. The word "model" is appropriate, even though Saint-Just used the present tense, as though he were describing an existing type of person. However, as one reads on through this long catalogue of personal qualities and ways of behaving, it becomes obvious that no existing person would be likely to possess all of them: "The revolutionary man [there is nothing here about women] is inflexible but reasonable; he is frugal; he is simple without parading the luxury of false modesty. . . . As his aim is to see the Revolution triumph, he never censures it, but he condemns its enemies without identifying it with them." Purity, Saint-Just continues, must govern the revolutionary's whole manner of communication: "Jealous of his purity [the revolutionary] watches himself when he speaks out of respect for it."[84] Though by no means the central theme in this speech, the notion of purity crops up again in contexts that reveal its importance as an idea he wants his audience of presumed fellow revolutionaries to grasp. Speaking about the issue of public disorder, he asserts, "Many people do not feel they have enough purity to seize crime hand to hand and doubt the supreme power of the truth." Amplifying this point, Saint-Just goes on to lament the disappearance of public conscience. In its disappearance he sees the source of social dissolution.[85]

In these examples purity apparently means the moral courage that comes from the absence of feelings of guilt, especially guilt that might inhibit the application of revolutionary justice. As we have seen and will see, anything that interfered with the application of revolutionary justice, a euphemism for the terror, was a constant preoccupation for Saint-Just.

Immediately after these lamentations about the decline of public morality, lamentations surprisingly similar to late-twentieth-century concerns, Saint-Just made an abrupt emotional reverse to soaring optimism about the future, an emotional reverse characteristic of revolutionary radicals, and not only such radicals.[86] He invoked the mission destiny had given to the present generation of the French people. After a few more shots at judges and police officers soft on crime (sic, *mollesse des juges*) and at criminal ambition, he worked his way to the "lessons of history and the mission granted by destiny to the present generation of the French people." These were the simple life for great men: "The cabins and the virtues are the grandeurs of the world."[87] No more palaces and courtesans after the Revolution!

The "lesson of history" for Saint-Just was that the road to a pure and simple society was far from easy and was fraught with dangers and temptations. As time passed, Saint-Just turned more and more towards administrative force, including terror, to bring about the desired revolution in morals. In an often quoted passage in this speech he first attacks arbitrary abuse by those in power, also one of his favorite themes: "We have no fatherland where the [government] minister . . . tears at the breast of his mother, when a clerk has the audacity of a sultan and conspires against public equality. Think only of fortifying this equality by the vehemence of a pure government which makes respect for all rights by means of a vast and judicious police." In advocating the "vehemence of a pure government," Saint-Just and the diminishing minority who supported his policy had arrived at Stalinism. An equally if not more appropriate simile would be the Chinese Legalists, who propounded in the third century B.C. a theory of rule by relentless force to create suitable subjects. By taking us backward in time and out of Western culture, the simile of the Legalists enables us to see that the issues faced by Saint-Just and by Stalin were not limited to their times and our culture.[88]

In the next to last sentence of this speech Saint-Just defined revolutionary government as "nothing else than justice favorable to the people and terrible to its enemies." There follows a decree made up of twenty-six articles. Their general purport is to tighten up and centralize further the machinery of government, giving the Committee of Public Safety more power and responsibility. Many of the articles reflect continuing if not increasing suspicion of conspiracies, despite the purported elimination of factions and conspiracies by their quite literal decapitation. Thus the first two articles require that persons arrested for conspiracy be brought before the revolutionary tribunal in Paris from all parts of the Republic. Likewise the Committees of Public Safety and General Security were to look promptly into the accomplices of the conspirators and have them brought before the revolutionary tribunal. Other articles imposed stricter rules, with some possible exceptions, on where former nobles might live. Articles 11–14 introduced a system of internal passports, probably just for former nobles and foreigners, though there is no definition of the "individuals" who will require them. Article 23 presents nicely the somewhat contradictory tone of the whole decree: "Henceforth anyone convicted of having complained about the Revolution [and] who lives without doing anything and is neither over 60 nor infirm, will be deported to Guiana."[89] Was there some hope for a society that legally exempted the old and the sick from the requirement of revolutionary enthusiasm?

If even a few scattered individuals hoped on the basis of this clause that exemption from the requirement of revolutionary enthusiasm might widen, subsequent events soon disappointed them. On June 10, 1794, partly in response to an attempt to assassinate Robespierre and Collot d'Herbois, a law known as the Law of 22 Prairial was passed.[90] The main purpose of the law was to facilitate and speed up the execution of "enemies of the people" in Paris, where this grisly task had been centralized. This the law did by stripping away the legal defenses of the accused and defining "enemy of the people" so broadly that it could cover just about anybody. As a result the number of death sentences soared. During the four winter months there were between 61 and 68 a month. In Prairial, the month of the new law, the number jumped to 509, and the following month, Messidor, to 796. In the first nine days of Thermidor alone there were 342 death sentences, a rate of over 1,000 a month had not Robespierre been overthrown.

There is no indication that Saint-Just played any role in the drafting of the Law of 22 Prairial. At that time he was away from Paris and with the victorious army of the north. He returned to Paris only on the night of June 28–29, 1794 (10–11 Messidor). On his return, however, he set to work at once, issuing death sentences as a major part of his task.[91]

During the spring of 1794 the meaning of terror for the revolutionary leadership—Robespierre, Saint-Just, and others—underwent an important set of changes. Terror, at its height already, became an instrument ostensibly for directed social change, the creation of a revolutionary man. In its latest form, however, the word "terror" disappeared, to be replaced by "justice." It was of course revolutionary justice, "favorable to the people and terrible to its enemies," as Saint-Just had put it in his speech of April 15, 1794.[92] Robespierre in the last weeks before his fall went so far as to utter sharp criticisms of terror in speeches before the Jacobins and the Convention.[93]

As mentioned above, Saint-Just energetically went to work enforcing his *justice terrible* on his return to Paris near the end of June 1794. And, as might be expected, justice terrible turned out in practice, and especially under pressure from Saint-Just, to

95

be a grisly, horrible form of injustice. The notorious case of the 159 prisoners from the Luxembourg prison, accused of conspiracy before the Revolutionary Tribunal, was a major example of justice terrible. The text of the accusations offered no evidence of conspiracy. It presented merely a miscellany of counterrevolutionary remarks overheard in the prison. Nevertheless, Saint-Just with others from the Committee of Public Safety on July 5, 1794, ordered all 159 prisoners turned over to the Revolutionary Tribunal, the equivalent of a death sentence. The public prosecutor feared that this was too big a "batch" (*fournée*) for public opinion to swallow, and asked that the batch be broken up into smaller limits to make the executions more palatable. Saint-Just objected. For him the collective execution appeared as an act of the justice terrible into which the terror was turning. The prosecutor, however, had his way. By dividing up the accused into three batches, he was able to slip in some individuals against whom there were no charges. Apparently this was the usual way to get rid of someone who seemed suspicious but against whom the evidence was weak or lacking. On July 7, 9, and 10, 1794, the prosecutor was able to put through the charges. All but 3 of the 159 were condemned to death. One of the 3 was a fourteen-year-old boy who received a sentence of "only" twenty years imprisonment.[94]

During these weeks that came to an end with the disintegration and death of the radical revolutionary leadership (9–10 Thermidor; July 27–28, 1794), there were several other episodes in which Saint-Just showed that for him justice terrible was a tool for moral cleansing, i.e., for the destruction of "enemies of the people."[95] But despite his energetic pursuit of what deserves to be called vindictive class-justice, there are strong indications that towards the end of his life he became aware that terror was no longer a weapon suitable for advancing the Revolution. Just when he made such remarks in notes to himself is uncertain.[96] Very likely Saint-Just wrote the notes after his return from the northern military front to Paris on the night of June 28–29, 1794. Immediately upon his return he was shocked by what he felt was the new and strange atmosphere in the Committee of Public Safety, now seething with half-concealed jealousies and fears of an imminent coup either for or against Robespierre. Some time after his return there seems to have been a current of opinion in the Committee of Public Safety to the effect that the terror had accomplished all it could, and that some other policy was necessary to push the Revolution forward. In notes that may have been jotted down in preparation for a report along these lines Saint-Just wrote:

> If there were morals *(moeurs)*, everything would go well; institutions are necessary to purify them. That's all one has to do. All the rest will follow.
>
> The terror can get rid of the monarchy and the aristocracy for us. But who will deliver us from corruption? . . . Some institutions. One has no doubt about this. One believes one has done everything when one has a machine for governing.[97]

Exactly what Saint-Just meant by institutions and how they were to work is very murky. Again he sounds like a 1920s political scientist designing machinery for a government that will never adopt it and would never work if it were adopted. But he was perfectly clear about what he wanted them to accomplish: a moral revolution in French society as a whole that would make corruption and other moral blemishes on the Revolution impossible. The mistake in revolutionary policy to date, Saint-Just came to believe, was the lack of any adequate effort to create a moral basis for the revolutionary Republic.[98] In a nutshell Saint-Just's message was: terror is not enough. So we need a moral revolution.

In another observation in his unpublished "Fragments," which must have been made after he had become familiar with the Parisian scene, his criticism of the terror was sharper: "The revolution is paralyzed *(glacée)*; all principles are enfeebled, all that remains are some revolutionary caps *(bonnets rouges)* worn for the sake of an intrigue. The terror has deadened the sense of crime just the way strong liquors deaden the palate."[99] This was a really extraordinary confession of failure by the man who could be considered the most outstanding leader of the Revolution next to Robespierre, and who was definitely the main theorist of terror. The confession was also an accurate if abbreviated explanation of the Revolution's collapse. The guillotine could not really purify French society or any other. Saint-Just may have been moving in a more promising direction in his stress on the need for a moral revolution. But by then the political situation made anything resembling a moral revolution out of the question.[100]

With his loss of faith in the currently existing Revolution, Saint-Just did not abandon his conceptions of purity as a method and purity as a goal for the Revolution. Saint-Just had never been one to enthuse at length about purity. Yet in his disgust at the loss of commitment to revolutionary ideals so visible in Paris, and even more so his distress over the intrigues and infighting within the Committee of Public Safety, which he did his very best to heal without success, the notion of purity did come to his mind and speech.[101]

His final speech to the Convention on July 27, 1794 (9 Thermidor, Year II), was strictly his own view of the dangerous situation into which the Revolution had fallen. Unlike his other speeches, he did not speak in the name of the Committee of Public Safety, whose internal fights he had not been able to overcome, and he did not clear the speech with colleagues. When he tried to give it before the Convention, he was interrupted after a few sentences, which did sound like the prelude to another purge of the Convention. Proscription lists were floating all over Paris at this time. Their authenticity was very doubtful, though it is clear that Robespierre wanted heads to roll at the apex of the government while refusing to name the intended victims. The interruption set off a general rout and hullabaloo on the floor of the Convention that ended with the arrest on the spot of Saint-Just and Robespierre, and their execution along with a few others. However the text has survived along with some notes for possible additional use.

The text itself is a curious mixture of descriptions and explanations of the disasters threatening the Revolution's top leadership, along with justifications for Saint-Just's own attempts to take a stand above the fray. Just before repeating rumors to the effect that some members of the Committee of Public Safety had bloody plans against other members so terrified that they dared not sleep in their own homes, Saint-Just expressed his independent disdain for such behavior: "I declare that one has tried to dissatisfy and envenom the minds in order to lead them to disastrous actions, and without doubt one has not hoped about me that I would lend my pure hands to iniquity."[102] In this context "pure" means "clean" in the sense of "innocent." Saint-Just is saying here that in his position of attempted peacemaker (revealed to be an utter failure as soon as he tried to deliver this speech), no one could expect him to dirty his hands by joining a murderous plot.

Another and far more important episode concerns the ending of this undelivered speech. As it stands, the text has a very flat and unimpressive ending. In the last sentence of the actual speech Saint-Just says he will not end by attacking those he has named; they should justify themselves so that all of us become wiser. There follows an utterly banal, proposed decree requiring the Convention to devise and refine institutions that will prevent the government from become arbitrary or repressive without losing any of its energy.[103] The night before, he had written out a much more dramatic ending, whose text has survived:

Detruisons les defiances ameres [accents omitted in original]
  occasionnées par le deffaut de sincerité,
Soyons Purs et Soyons grands, Soyons genereux,
  Soyons sages.

[Let us destroy the bitter distrusts brought about by the
  absence of sincerity,
Let us be pure, let us be great, let us be generous,
  let us be wise.][104]

Is it sheer accident that purity is the first quality to be mentioned in the final peroration? I rather think not, because in his whole career Saint-Just put revolutionary purity first.

Though he never had a chance to speak these moving lines, and quite possibly under the circumstances never wanted to, his last public appearance was in itself a dramatic conclusion to his career. After his speech had been interrupted, he stood nonchalantly leaning against the lectern, seemingly unaware of the tumult around him. From time to time he cast a disdainful glance at the principal actors on this fateful day. But never once did he try to speak. One of his enemies observing the scene was deeply impressed and had this to say about his behavior, "He preserved his dignity while losing all hope."[105] The next day he went before the guillotine. Contrary to the usual practice the execution took place on a *Décadi,* the revolutionary substitute for a Sunday. That enabled enormous crowds to attend the theatrical festival, screaming their insults and cries of victory at the victims being driven in carts to the guillotine. Alone among the victims, according to a contemporary witness, Saint-Just still maintained an attitude of calm and contemptuous detachment.[106]

THE TRANSFORMATIONS OF MONOTHEISM

We have reached the end of our soundings into the history of Jewish and Christian monotheism in their political aspects. It is appropriate therefore to undertake a brief sketch of the transformations of monotheism from the times of the Old Testament through the turmoil of the French Revolution and beyond. The transformations appear most clearly in the social goals, the historically changing "happy ending" or "happily forever after" that monotheism is expected to bring about. This utopian or near-utopian aspect of monotheism has been a major source of the dynamism and tragedy of Western civilization.

Realistic gradualism—step by step improvement taken with due care to stay within the limits of socially defined possibility—can be much less traumatic for a people undergoing a major historical change such as the intrusion of modern technology into a peasant society. However, it is very difficult to see how realistic gradualism alone can ever seriously reduce the structural suffering inherent in corrupt and oppressive capitalist dictatorial regimes, and corrupt and oppressive socialist dictatorial regimes. These two types of regimes rule over a huge majority of the world's populations. The happy ending and ways to get there—or avoid trying to get there—have made and still make a huge difference in human suffering. That there has never been a real happy ending, not even in the economically advanced countries—in the sense of no more large pockets of poverty, limited prospects, general dissatisfaction—is obvious enough to make comment superfluous. Oddly enough, the failure of happy endings assures militant and repressive movements a flourishing future. It is success that kills them off, when it does occur.

In the Old Testament the rewards for good behavior ("good behavior" meaning sticking to the rituals of monotheism at home and slaying the enemies of monotheism abroad) are at first reassuringly materialistic. The ancient Hebrews could expect to live in a rich land flowing with milk and honey after their captivity in Egypt and subsequent wanderings and battles. Virtuous orthodoxy was by no means merely its own reward. Instead it paid off in good real estate and numberless progeny to care for flocks and crops. The word went around: "Be fruitful and multiply." Fine advice as long as there was no surplus of labor. With defeats by foreign enemies, the loss of the Ark of the Covenant and the destruction of the Temple, the publicly expressed mood became more somber and more wistful. There was much longing for the recovery and restoration of the Temple that had housed the Ark. Though such longings may seem pathetic and unrealistic to foreigners centuries later, the rediscovery of the Ark and the recovery of the Temple were expected to take place on this earth, if at some uncertain date. The Messiah was to appear *here*, if by no means *now*. It might be necessary to wait a very long time for the return of Israel's glory and the monotheism that supposedly guaranteed it, but, unless I have missed some passage, it was not postponed to the next world, or after death. That was the contribution of Christianity.

101

And it came about only after the Kingdom of Heaven failed to materialize on earth.

The growth of Christianity out of Judaism had several very significant consequences. First of all, it spread monotheism, with its inherent conflicts, over a vastly greater geographical area. Secondly, it moved the happy ending and its opposite, eternal suffering in Hell, clearly and definitely into the life after death. That move raised the stakes all around. It was much more important to avoid eternal damnation than to wait somewhat uneasily for the Messiah and a happy ending on this earth. Thirdly, the large number of diverse peoples brought into the orbit of monotheism released conflicts about just what monotheism meant anyway, the proper forms of worship, and what just one god could do for the individual worshiper. Under one god and eternal damnation the pagan solution of adding another special-purpose deity when needed or continually expanding the attributes and powers of gods already available were ruled out. The result was a series of conflicts, often bloody, in which a vindictive, self-righteous defense, the "pure" religion, played an important part. Important though this factor was, one must not ignore others. The Crusades were driven by cupidity as well as Christianity. For that matter one can have institutionalized and state-supported cruelty on a huge scale under paganism and without the self-righteous belief in a single god. The gladiatorial shows in Rome and its provincial cities are a well-known example. Their main purpose was merely entertainment, hence essentially secular.

The fourth and so far the most important transformation of monotheism was the secularization of this impulse as part of the rationalist and critical trend toward religion and the supernatural in eighteenth-century French thought. This movement, which culminated in the radical paroxysm that ended the French Revolution and left a baleful influence in subsequent centuries, was never absolutely complete. There was, for instance, Robespierre's much-mocked Festival of Reason and, apart from radicalism, the relatively peaceful current of Deism that has also influenced respectable religion down to the present day. Were it not for the continuation of the religious impulses, to speak of secular monotheism might seem a contradiction in terms. However, the language is of no great importance. We are interested in what people actually said and did, not in definitions of their behavior.

The behaviors that surfaced in the French Revolution were the familiar ones of militant monotheism. There was the usual demonization and dehumanization of actual and potential opponents. Revolutionaries perceived them as outsiders, threats to human society who should be expelled and killed. A substantial number, the inhabitants of the Vendée for instance, were social outsiders to begin with. Aristocrats and the well-to-do, against whom latent hostility increased to hatred, became "enemies of the people" and thereby demonized by the internal dynamic of the Revolution. This process of creating legitimate internal targets appears to have been relatively new and especially ominous. In earlier persecutions the "outsiders" were often ready made into what Max Weber referred to as "pariah peoples," Jews and Kurds, or Canaanites and Philistines, competitors for the same land. That one's own society could secrete moral pollution seems to have been a new idea, at least in terms of the degree of emphasis it received.

There was a hoped-for happy ending to the sufferings of the French Revolution in the petit bourgeois, egalitarian utopia of Robespierre, which eventually transmuted into the device "Liberty, Equality, Fraternity." Still safely remote from reality, the device records an important victory over the Old Regime's system of status. For Saint-Just and many like him the happy ending would also have to bring corruption under control. Saint-Just had no idea how to achieve this. That is not surprising since the problem was enormous in the eighteenth century. Corruption was rampant all across Europe, from England to and including Russia. The great Russian historian Kliuchevskii has a vivid account of the corruption and political disintegration facing Catherine the Great as she began to take power in the early

1760s.[107] (Russia was a kleptocracy diluted by anarchy and incompetence at that point in her history too.)

Saint-Just and his like might just possibly have had some inkling of the extent of European corruption in their day, though accurate knowledge of foreign countries was not a revolutionary strong point. But they could not possibly have anticipated the way corruption became manageable: through the nonrevolutionary and even antirevolutionary currents of moral sobriety, accuracy, and devotion to duty that surged through England and Germany and to a lesser extent other states during the nineteenth century.[108] Instead of these, Robespierre, Saint-Just, and even Carnot for a short time resorted to the guillotine as *the* instrument for transforming society. Thus, the vindictive and cruel persecution of their opponents, along with the demonization of their enemies, appears in an intensified form among the key leaders of the French Revolutionary radicals. There is plenty of evidence for the same traits among the self-appointed yet very popular spokesmen for the sans-culottes up until the time when the Revolution literally and figuratively decapitated them.

Vindictive persecution, justified and encouraged by varying forms of monotheism and moral absolutism, is a frightening trend that now permeates Western civilization. In the next and final chapter we shall undertake a bird's-eye tour of the main Asiatic religions to determine the extent, if any, of similar social trends existing there.

Notes on Purity and Pollution
in Asiatic Civilizations

HINDU CASTE

THE HINDU caste system is a hierarchical ordering of the population into endogamous groups based on a scale with purity at the top and disgust or impurity at the bottom. The Brahmins at the top are the "most pure of men," while the Untouchables are the least pure.[1]

The whole system rests upon its bottom layers, the Untouchables, also known in modern times as Harijans and Scheduled Castes, as well as Outcastes. The plural "layers" is appropriate because by the beginning of the Christian era the Untouchables had created a caste system of their own, including their own outcastes. Later on, every Untouchable group imagined that there was another group lower than itself.[2] In this way a society based on inequality could gain in stability by making it possible for everybody to feel superior to somebody.

The Untouchables were for the most part excluded from the larger Aryan society made up of the twice-born castes: Brahmins (priests), kshatriya (warriors and rulers), and vaisya (merchants). Yet even if excluded and humiliated, the Untouchables were also part of Hindu society insofar as they performed tasks essential to the status of the higher castes.

The Untouchables did the hard and dirty work for the upper castes, and continue this service to a great extent even now. In recent times large numbers have been serving as landless laborers. In pre-British times their main task was the cremation of human corpses. They also served as executioners.[3] Their arduous and repulsive labors enabled the Brahmins to live purely. There is nothing exotic or especially Hindu about this arrangement. The division of labor all over the world displays roughly similar features.

Untouchables were kept at arm's length from the twice-born castes,[4] ostensibly on account of pollution from contact with dead bodies. For this reason Untouchables were also leather workers. They were not allowed to live in an Aryan town or village. Instead they had special quarters outside of town or village boundaries. No higher-caste man could have any but the most distant relations with an Untouchable on pain of losing his religious purity. On entering a town, an Untouchable, like a European leper, was forced to strike a wooden clapper to warn Aryans against his polluting approach.[5]

As is widely recognized, Hindu religion lacks any dogma or core of central beliefs to which all Hindus are expected to adhere. That once meant there could be no such thing as a pure Hinduism, one that could be defended by force of arms, if necessary, as in the great religious struggles from which Western society— and, to a lesser extent, Islam—have suffered from the time of the Old Testament onward. In practice, Hinduism has for some time been extremely tolerant. Any new idea or religious ritual becomes the basis for a new caste. But the tolerance extends further than that to just about any form of deviant behavior. There are even criminal castes "whose hereditary occupation is crime." Such castes offer prayers to their special divinity before setting out on expeditions of armed robbery and murder. Crime, for these castes, is believed to be under divine favor. If it is not practiced, a man may suffer from divine anger.[6] With a society that could not, in its original state, generate religious persecution and religious warfare, Hinduism stumbled into the acceptance of organized crime, which has probably caused its own brand of substantial suffering, even if less than that caused by religious warfare and persecution in the West.

Looking at Hindu society around 1910, when English power seemed firmest, one might have found a strange anomaly. Here was a society organized around feelings of impurity, pollution, and disgust, yet remarkably tolerant. With a closer look the contradictions disappear. The Hindu caste system accepted people who did disgusting things and therefore became polluting, but it kept such people apart from the rest of Hindu society as much as possible. Thus, the welcome actually meant acceptance at the bottom of a stifling hierarchy. Nor was Hinduism's tolerant welcome by any means universal. The Islamic conquerors were hardly absorbed, even if they were to a degree compelled to be just another caste. As for Europeans, especially the British with their repulsive fondness for steak and liquor, Hindu officials who could not avoid dealings with them found it necessary to undergo a complex purification after each discussion. Finally, the shared institution of caste and religious tolerance did nothing to stop the murderous little wars among kinglets and chieftains. The British stopped them. Natives could not or would not. All these factors eventually helped produce a favorable reception for an antiforeign, superpatriotic movement in the last quarter of the twentieth century.

Meanwhile a very large body of "ordinary" Hindus have learned in recent times to overcome the tradition of tolerance and have taken up a neofascist form of nationalism, manifested in violent attacks on Muslim monuments and a general hatred of Islam and, later, Christianity. On this score it is reasonably plain that Hinduism learned religious hatred in response to the Muslim conquest and the establishment of the Muslim Empire in northern India during the sixteenth century. Just how much Hindu hostility there was to the Islamic rulers with their conciliatory policy is hard to ascertain. In any case Hindu-Islamic hostilities simmered noisily under British rule, to burst forth in horrible slaughter in connection with Partition in 1947.

Recollecting these events is more than enough to show that Hindu hatred of Islam is nothing new as such and has well-nourished roots in India's history and social structure. But the turn towards a politically prominent neofascism is new. It is part of a widespread disenchantment with Nehru's secularist semisocialism, which failed to generate enough welfare while supposedly coddling Islamic minorities and Scheduled Castes.[7] Such policies are rather ordinary, standard Semifascist Fare. The striking feature of Hindu semifascism is its ability to tap and mobilize traditional fears of sacrilege and disgust. All castes in "traditional" India had intense fears of this sort. Rules of endogamy, diet, and intercaste etiquette kept them under control. These aspects come to light most vividly in the notorious Hindu attack on a famous mosque allegedly erected on the birthplace of the Hindu god Ram.[8] For a Westerner, the event brings to mind the Nazi attack on Jews in the infamous *Kristallnacht* (from the glass broken by Nazi thugs) shortly before the beginning of World War II.

Disturbing though the similarities are, they do not convey the real meaning of the events just sketched here, a meaning that seems to me more significant and sadder. If one could go back to examine the Hindu social order in the early eighteenth century, when that of the Muslim rulers had collapsed and that of the British had yet to be established, there is one point on which there would have been widespread agreement: the Hindu social order is *not* a social order liable to generate a militant cult of moral purity justifying a punitive cruelty towards what are defined as strangers and foreigners. (Scheduled Castes have been correctly defined as Hindu, and efforts made—without much success—to include them in a nationalist and patriotic front.) Yet a movement of militant moral purity has become a major feature in Indian politics despite these unpromising conditions. Again, two factors produced it: the Islamic conquest in the first place, and the failure of Nehru's semisocialism to satisfy large sectors of the population in the second place. There is nothing recondite or unusual about this combination of circumstances. It could occur anywhere. Evidently it is not *that* hard to introduce systematic and morally justified cruelty into the mores of a civilization where the undertaking looks unpromising. Eliminating such cruelty is possible, but vastly harder.

BUDDHISM

From the standpoint of this inquiry, Buddhism is significant because it generated both a conception of moral purity and of Hell to support it, yet did not create a theory and practice of militant moral purification comparable to those widespread in Western civilization. To understand this seemingly paradoxical development it will be necessary to review briefly the main outlines of Buddhist history.

Buddhism began partly as an egalitarian reaction against the Hindu caste system, though this aspect soon fell into the background. The founder of the new religion, Siddhartha Gautama, flourished during the fifth century B.C. and thus was a contemporary of Socrates.[9] In due course the doctrines crystallized in the written form known as Theravada Buddhism, or Buddhism of the Elders. The main doctrines that have been central to Buddhism, though modifications and additions came later, were these: (1) the rejection of extreme self-punitive asceticism as a technique for salvation and (2) the Four Noble Truths, which together hold that all of life, even its passionate delights, are but a source of sorrow. According to the Fourth Noble Truth, ending the craving for life so that no passion remains is the only way to stop the suffering. This point is elaborated in the Noble Eightfold Path, eight rules of correct conduct and correct speech that exemplify morally approved conduct in most cultures and require no elaboration here.[10] Since life is full of suffering, the main object in life, one can say in summarizing Buddhism very briefly, is to escape from the endless series of birth and rebirths posited by Hinduism, and achieve Nirvana. In most Buddhist texts, though not all, Nirvana is simply the end of all sensations. To my mind Nirvana so described is simply another word for death (a conclusion against which friends knowledgeable about Buddhism are inclined to bridle).[11]

Be that as it may, the extreme pessimism of Theravada Buddhism is a very significant feature. At the start, of course, Buddhism presents itself as more hopeful than Hinduism because it rejects the rigidities of caste and the endless cycle of rebirths. Yet, what did Buddhism offer in its place? An individual who worked really hard at following the Noble Eightfold Path of conventional virtues might expect what? Death.

There may be some connection between this extreme pessimism in Buddhism and the very weak development of binary
notions of purity like the blessed and the damned so prominent
in the West and Middle East. If even the most orthodox and
most holy face nothing better than oblivion at the end of life's
bitter road, how can one single them out as a certified model for
the rest of human society?

If Buddhism had been the carrier of no more than this very
pessimistic, elitist, and individualist tradition of salvation as death,
it is unlikely that it could have achieved the status of a world religion. But change it did, in ways that greatly increased its popular appeal. Two doctrinal innovations were especially significant. One was the creation of a host of semidivine creatures, the
bodhisattvas, full of compassion for fallible ordinary mortals.
This emphasis on compassion and peace is the distinctive moral
aspect of Buddhism. The other innovation was much less significant generally, yet important for the purposes of this inquiry:
the development of a Pure Land school of Buddhism, where the
notion of purity was the object of considerable attention and
elaboration.

In the course of the first century A.D., Buddhism underwent
what we can fairly call a democratic transformation and, according to its official doctrine, spread to China. What connection there may have been between these two events is unclear
and unimportant for our purposes.[12] It is likely that even in Buddha's lifetime he was considered the last of a series of earlier
Buddhas. Later, possibly under Zoroastrian influence, the belief
arose that other Buddhas were yet to come. An interest developed in the *Maetreya*, the future Buddha to appear in years to
come and purify the world. But if the Maetreya was yet to come,
his soul must already be in existence and active for the good of
mankind. And if this one, how many more? The world must be
full of bodhisattvas, all striving for the welfare of other beings.[13]

The discovery or invention of the bodhisattvas produced a de-
mocratization of the Buddhist movement by changing the technique of salvation. Under the older Therevada Buddhism the

road to salvation was an unaided struggle for individual perfection. *Arhats,* or "worthies" (also *arhant*), were individuals who had become perfected beings already enjoying Nirvana. This goal began to be looked upon as selfish. A bodhisattva having reached perfection would not pass so quickly to Nirvana, where such a being could be of no further help to humanity. Instead this semidivine creature would deliberately choose to stay in the world, using its spiritual power to help others until all had found salvation. The replacement of the individualist arhant with the self-sacrificing bodhisattvas marks the basic distinction between the older Buddhism and the newer one, known as the Mahayana, or Greater Vehicle.[14]

In Buddhism the search for purity and salvation was not a special privilege or task for the elect, as it was under Calvinism and, in a secular version, under French revolutionary radicalism. Instead the Buddhist quest was, at least in theory, panhuman. This panhuman aim for purity and salvation may be a reason for the absence of cruel struggles over dogma under Buddhism despite the luxuriant flourishing of sects and accusations of heresy. There were other reasons too that we shall examine in due course.

According to the fully developed Mahayanist cosmology, the heavenly Buddha chiefly concerned with our world was called "Immeasurable Radiance" and lived in the "Pure Land," as it was known to the Chinese ("Happy Land" or "Heaven of the West" to non-Chinese).[15] Discussion of the Pure Land should reveal more fully than any other doctrinal expositions just what the Buddhists had in mind when they were discussing purity.

The Pure Land sect appealed especially to the practical-minded Chinese, with their strong dose of syncretism that enabled them to fit a new idea in somewhere among previous beliefs without undue trouble.[16] Indeed, the complex and incomprehensible nature of Buddhist doctrine, very likely the most aridly convoluted theology of any major religion, persuaded many clerics and laymen that their only hope rested in salvation by faith in the saving power of Buddha. Such was the

111

impulse behind the *Pure Land Scripture,* one of the principal texts of Pure Land salvationism.

According to this text, Amita, the heavenly Buddha chiefly concerned with this world (also known as Amitabha), who dwelt in the Pure Land,[17] while still a bodhisattva took forty-eight vows that were instrumental in his attainment of buddhahood. In accord with widespread Buddhist practice it appears that Amita performed the heavy drudgery of gaining salvation from which others might benefit. Hence the simple ejaculation of Amita's name (in Chinese, A-mi-to-fo) "became the most common of all religious practices in China, and the means by which millions sought release from the sufferings of this world." According to one commentary, the purity of the Amita Buddha's adornments meant that, unlike ordinary secular ones, they were not subject to corruption and contamination.[18]

What about the Pure Land itself? It is Paradise and therefore, of course, imaginary. It seems to have replaced Nirvana as the final focus or state of salvation, though I have not come upon a specific text supporting this judgment. At any rate the Pure Land is definitely the place where the cares and frustrations of life in this world have ceased to plague human beings. There is choice of hot and cold running water in the rivers, fine food, a perfumed ambiance, but no sex. In fact one of its claimed advantages was the absence of moral temptation such as women.[19] According to Conze's commentary on the *Diamond Sutra,* "In a 'Pure Land' [apparently there can be several] all is beauty and order." It contrasts sharply with "an ordinary, defiled world such as ours." Thus, for Buddhists as for us, purity contrasts with defilement. But for Buddhists purity also connotes not only beauty but also comfort and satisfaction of the senses. Bodhisattvas "can bring to perfection a heaven or paradise that offers ideal conditions for rapid spiritual progress."[20] Thus a Pure Land is definitely an imaginary land of moral purity.

This is a good place to bring together a few other remarks about purity to round out our account of Buddhist conceptions of this topic. Unlike the phenomena of what we might call the

112

secular world, for Buddhists purity is not subject to corruption.[21] There is a fundamental difference from Western doctrines here. In the West we come upon frequent anxieties about the erosion of purity and its decay. Quite noticeable in the case of an alleged decline of revolutionary purity and a turn towards corruption, the same phenomenon occurs in a religious context as well. Under Buddhism the theoretical impossibility of evasion and decay removes a major ground for religious quarrels and persecution.

However, Buddhists seem to have found a way to get around this obstacle to the enforcement of religious orthodoxy, which in any case appeared to have been a rather secondary concern. The way was quite simple: a few ideas and forms of behavior were labeled as criminal. Just when and how this happened is not clear, though the prohibitions seem to go back as far as the time of the original Buddha. The prohibitions are known as the Five Violations and the Ten Evils. The fifteen prohibitions include striking a Buddha so that he bleeds, and the usual set of prohibitions found in literate cultures and complex societies: patricide, matricide, murder of an arhant, killing, stealing, adultery, lying, duplicity, slander, obscene language, lust, anger, and false views. Sanctions supporting the social necessity of all these prohibitions occur in most human cultures. Under Buddhism the penalty for violating these prohibitions was an endless sojourn in the "Hell of Uninterrupted Suffering."[22] As similar Western experience demonstrates, with the conception of Hell Buddhism found a very useful adjunct to its theories of moral impurity. Presumably not every penalty was delayed until the next world when the Hell of Uninterrupted Suffering took over. There must have been incorrigible individuals and heinous crimes for which an immediate and severe response was deemed necessary. But on that issue the text is silent.

Buddhism recognized the distinction between clean and unclean things. Unclean means disgusting, as with dung, urine, spittle, pus, and blood.[23] However, unlike the ancient Hebrews of the Old Testament, Buddhists did not rear an elaborate structure of fears, beliefs, and taboos on this recognition.

113

On the other hand, the Buddhists faced plenty of reasons for fear and anxiety anyway. They put the load of these fears on the bodhisattvas. Their obligation was to save the whole world from the "forest of births, old age, disease, rebirths, . . . misfortune and sin, . . . the rounds of birth and death, from the toils of heresy."[24] Evidently the Buddhists had a concept of heresy, or at least a word that could be translated that way. But as in the case of "unclean," there was no sign of theological and political elaboration of this basic awareness. Instead there was enormous elaboration of a metaphysical theology, twirling about every conceivable attachment point like a sickly vine that bears neither fruit nor flower. But if Buddhists bored people to death, which is not certain, at least they did not burn people for their opinions.

In concluding, we may take a second look at Buddhist doctrines to find those aspects that hindered or prevented the development of a militant, persecuting variant of moral purity. The main ingredients for persecution were present. Buddhists believed in moral purity, the distinction between clean and unclean, and displayed a highly punitive attitude towards major moral lapses such as adultery, lying, stealing, and physical attack on a Buddha. Why, then, did Buddhism fail to develop an ethic of persecuting purity?

One of the more obvious reasons is that from the beginning the main object of Buddhist religion was to escape from this worldly life, to achieve Nirvana, rather than to reorder life in this world by something similar to a moral revolution.[25] To be sure, the emphasis in both Western religion and Buddhism was on the life to come. But what was expected and hoped for in the meantime was very different.

In Buddhist cosmology all things are composite and transient. They have no eternal self. The personality is in a constant state of flux. There is no such thing as an eternal soul. All that is a fundamental illusion.[26] This set of ideas amounts to a complete denial of Platonism. To take this anti-Platonism seriously, to deny the very possibility of pure essences, and yet construct a doctrine claiming a purity relevant for this world would be impossible. Buddhists limited purity to bodhisattvas, beings partly divine and partly human. In contrast to Western monotheistic religions, Indian systems of belief mingled divine and human qualities. By itself this mingling would render difficult any concept of divine purity. On that score the relative tolerance of polytheism in comparison with monotheism is too well known to require elaboration here. But in the case of bodhisattva-purity there is an even more important difference from Western theory and practice. Bodhisattvas embodied what we may fairly call Buddhist surplus compassion as an ideal major emphasis in this culture. Supposedly, under Mahayana or "democratic" Buddhism the world was full of bodhisattvas striving for the welfare of other beings.[27] In other words the moral purity that a bodhisattva had acquired with great effort was to be used to make other people happier or at least less miserable. It was definitely not to be used as a source of pride in one's distinctive virtue vis-à-vis other human beings or as a moral justification for cleaning out and destroying the morally impure and corrupt elements in society.

Even in Theravada Buddhism there is the same compassionate desire for the welfare of all living things, presumably including the poisonous ones. According to their morality one should never injure, kill, put in bonds, or do other acts of violence.[28] There is not to be any hatred. But as the editor observes, there are few outright condemnations of warfare in Buddhist literature.[29] Furthermore, there have been a scattering of warrior monasteries in the course of Buddhist history, and at times they have played a leading role in warfare.[30] Such evidence leads to the suspicion that under certain modern circumstances, say, a Buddhist ruling-class faced with a guerrilla threat by a religious and ethnic minority, all the attractive moral dykes against violent persecution would dissolve like a sand castle in a hurricane.

CONFUCIAN CHINA

From the beginning on down through some three thousand years of recorded history, Confucianism failed to generate within its ranks any sustained militant movement for moral purity *and* the persecution of the impure. Movements for moral reform within the governing stratum of scholar-officials did appear frequently, but this was moral tinkering rather than moral cleansing. In fact there was a great deal of moral concern in dynastic China. Confucianism was a great advocate of patriarchal morality, in the hope that it might keep a frequently turbulent population quiet and generate an economic surplus for the elite. It is not too much of an exaggeration to call the Confucian system government by edification, flavored with brutality.

As might be anticipated, it did not work very well, even though it lasted such a long time. It was subject to periodic breakdown when a dynasty weakened and the populace revolted. When that happened, the imperial forces could be fierce in their defense of Confucianism. It would be correct to consider this often brutal defense persecution on behalf of Confucianism. But these were defensive actions, not efforts to purify or spread Confucianism. The secret societies that often played a major catalytic role in popular rebellions may have come closer to a movement for moral purity. They were of course hostile to Confucianism and claimed an otherworldly sanction for their actions, stigmata also characteristic of Western movements for religious opposition and moral purity.[31] Since our concern here is with Confucianism and its attitude, or lack of one, towards moral purity, there is no reason to look further into these movements.

Two famous episodes in Chinese history constituted a close call in avoiding a well-rooted theory and practice of militant moral purity. In the earlier episode, which occurred in 213 B.C., China acquired the dubious distinction of being, to my limited knowledge, the first civilized state to burn books and slaughter intellectuals. That was part of the work of China's extraordinary first emperor, who by military force created a new state out of a collection of small ones fighting each other and known as the Warring States. His treatment of books and intellectuals—more exactly, scholars—was part of his endeavor to wipe out the past and make a fresh start with a strictly disciplined, autocratic state.

The effort failed. His one-man dynasty, the Ch'in (whence China), rapidly disintegrated upon his death. The dynasty ruled for only fourteen years, from 221 to 207 B.C.[32] The net effect of the first emperor's acts and failure was to create a model memory of what a dynastic government must not do. It must not burn the books. It must not slaughter scholars. It must not try to wipe out the past. Instead, it should cherish books and scholars, and preserve the past in order to learn from it. Succeeding dynasties did borrow some of the first emperor's reliance on stiff rules. But no subsequent ruler tried to impose a quasi-totalitarian discipline on the Chinese population. One simple reason goes a long way toward explaining this restraint. China was just too big and the administrative staff was much too small to consider anything of the sort. Experience and geography together inoculated China against this form of plague.

The second episode, which occurred several centuries later, was more threatening, enough so to make a detached observer wonder if the inoculating had really taken hold. The reasons for this wondering come, of course, from European experience. Persecution often arises against a minority religious group that challenges the unchallengeable dogma of the majority. On both sides the issue becomes one of blasphemy. Both sides claim to be advocates of moral purity. In France this dynamic played itself out in the conflict between the Huguenots and the Catholics and earlier in the persecution of the Cathari. The Jews were caught up in it all over Europe, though the intensity of the dynamic varied greatly with time and place.

For a time during the latter part of the T'ang dynasty (A.D. 618–906) the situation looked as though the dynamic might take hold in China, with Buddhism playing the role of persecuted minority, albeit a large and powerful one. In 844–845 the one major religious persecution in all of Chinese history is reported to have laid waste 40,000 Buddhist temples and 4,600 monasteries.[33] It seems likely that the Chinese authorities were more concerned about the growth of an *imperium in imperio* and the consequent loss of tax revenues than the Buddhist doctrinal challenge. This

117

impression gains strength from the fact that there was consider-able religious syncretism at the time. Buddhist monks studied the Confucian classics.[34] In other words there was little or no hiving off into opposing forms of doctrinal and moral purity such as took place on the continent in western Europe.

The destruction of the temples and monasteries was not the end of Buddhism, though it seriously weakened it. Instead it was the beginning of a more persistent persecution. At that time the Buddhist threat was a major source of Chinese fears for the sur-vival of the nation, fears supposedly based on an over-ready ac-ceptance of alien cultural influences. These concerns became prominent at the breakup of the T'ang dynasty, and under the succeeding period of the Five Dynasties (907–960) the idea took root that a multiplicity of worldviews could not exist side by side. This idea bloomed under the next dynasty, the Sung (960–1280), known as the "most Confucian of all ages."[35] In other words there was a powerful resurgence of Confucian self-confidence. The Sung were known not only for their Confucianism but also for artistic achievements that have made the dynasty appear to some as the apex of Chinese cultural achievement. Meanwhile Bud-dhism continued a decline begun centuries earlier. Thus the events just described left China a remarkably homogeneous soci-ety. By about that time there were no internal enemies worth fear-ing and hating.

How about the foreign barbarians? By then China had man-aged to throw off threatening divisive trends and assert proudly its Confucian identity. It is reasonable to expect under these conditions an intensified hostility to foreigners, based on claims to moral and cultural superiority. Something of the sort did hap-pen, but in a way that undercuts the prospects for any xeno-phobic moral crusade. After the Sung, foreigners conquered China twice. The Mongol conquest produced the Yüan dynasty (1250–1368) and the Manchu conquest led to the founding of China's last dynasty, the Ch'ing (1644–1912). In both cases the new conquering rulers were rapidly Sinicized, though some ceremonial distinctions did remain. The absorption of the foreigners by China was by no means just a matter of cultural imperialism.

From the standpoint of the conqueror it was a matter of being practical. The only way to run China before the age of rapid transit (which has yet to arrive at the end of the twentieth century) appears to have been with an emperor and a provisionally loyal body of scholar-officials. If there was another way, the conquerors did not find it, and most likely wasted little time trying to find one. In this situation a foreign dynasty—and two of the last three were foreign—would risk alienating its new Chinese subjects and the foreigners from whom it stemmed by any vigorous policy of expansion justified by moral purity. Such a justification wouldn't make sense. Hence, real burning hostility to "foreign devils" did not put in an appearance until the intrusion of the West in the nineteenth century, events that lie outside the limits of this study.

Even if the conditions for exercising a self-serving, angry moral purity were unfavorable, the question remains: Did Confucianism ever develop a body of ideas and practices we can recognize as a cult of moral purity? The issue is not just a matter of language and translation, important though these can be. It is also very much a question of behavior. For example, well-known Chinese thinkers might or might not have an expression close to moral purity, with its divine or transcendental sanctions, as in the Western cases discussed earlier. Further, we have to find out if prominent thinkers, not just isolated marginal writers, expressed fears of impurity, contamination, and pollution similar to those found in the Western cases and widely known to permeate Western culture since then. In other words we are trying to find out if a whole Western complex of ideas and behavior had a rough counterpart in dynastic China, as well as what might be missing and why.

To avoid misapprehensions about this comparison that I have encountered orally from time to time, a few remarks may be helpful before examining some primary Chinese texts. One objection goes somewhat like this: "Why should anyone expect moral purity in Chinese culture? Isn't that just a concealed form of Western chauvinism and imperialism?" The answer to this objection is a simple, empirical one: it is impossible to tell what the facts are without looking for them. An ideological position that tries in this way to trivialize potentially important facts is merely a modern form of obscurantism. A diametrically opposite objection goes roughly as follows: "In making such a comparison, isn't one merely slandering Western culture and idealizing the Chinese?" The two objections cancel each other out. Hence the reply to the first one covers both. Let us then proceed to the analysis of some major Chinese texts that have both reflected Chinese elite culture and shaped its content.

The *Analects* of Confucius purport to record the sayings of a sage by that name who flourished towards the end of the sixth century B.C. and the first twenty years of the fifth. The compilation took place long after his death, at a time when several disciples already had schools of their own. Not until the second century A.D. did the text receive something like its present form.[36] Hence it is virtually impossible to determine exactly what Confucius did and did not say. Fortunately for our purposes, that does not make a particle of difference. Written as a guide to the ethics and etiquette of a bureaucracy that did not yet exist, the *Analects* later became *the* handbook of the scholar-officials, who were required to be familiar with it until the formal abolition of the imperial examination system in 1905 under the last dynasty.

In the whole text of the *Analects,* 169 aphoristic pages in this English version, a word based on purity occurs only once at VII, 12. The Chinese language evidently did have an expression that Waley, a superb translator, renders with the English word "purification." Used only once, the concept seems very far from salient. The compilers and author or authors do not appear very concerned with the issues raised by the term.

One has to be careful here, nevertheless, because the Chinese may have used words other than purity to convey a very similar idea. In reviewing the *Analects* once more, I came upon three relevant references, including the one just mentioned: VII, 12 refers to rites of "purification before sacrifice with war, and with sickness." Second, the last sentence of VIII, 4 refers to ritual specialists whose services one ordered when necessary, but this time without mentioning purification. Ritual purity, of course, was very important in ancient societies and many nonliterate ones. We shall come back to it in the Chinese context at an appropriate point.

For now let us examine the remaining third set of passages in the *Analects,* IV, 5, 6, the most interesting ones partly because they are the most ambiguous. Too long for quotation here, they are a series of comments on what a Chinese gentleman could be expected to fear and avoid and, at less length, what he should hope and strive for. The negative aspects are plain enough: poverty, obscurity, wickedness. But what about the positive one "goodness." Presumably the absence of the negative traits—or at least of wickedness—is at least part of goodness. But there is more. At the beginning of IV, 6, Confucius is quoted as saying he had "never yet seen one who really cared for goodness, nor one who really abhorred wickedness." Thus the expectation of a serious moral struggle between vice and virtue was attributed to Confucius and made its way into the canon. The Confucian gentleman was no Calvinist with his daily *examen de conscience.* Yet the Confucian internal moral struggle sounds intense in this passage. If successful, what were supposed to be the results? Can goodness mean anything more than the conquest and control of the usual forms of wickedness in Chinese society? And doesn't this amount to moral purity? Perhaps. Psychologically demanding it may have been, but there is no sign here of a vigorous search for converts or a punitive attitude toward unbelievers.

One last comment before we move on to a later and quite different phase of Confucianism. In the *Analects* the rites appear highly charged with moral significance and power. For Confucius, according to Bauer, "Ritual still had the function of utilizing age-old practices such as sacrifices and the cult of the dead, which had lost much of their meaning as Confucius put living man at the center of intellectual concern."[37] In these early days of lively philosophical debate, long before Confucianism had congealed into the official doctrine of an increasingly autocratic state, Hsün-tzu (?298–238 B.C.), a very able and hardheaded opponent of Confucian doctrine, held, again according to Bauer, that ritual was the means by which human beings tamed the beast in man and wrested oases of culture from the endless, brutal cycle of life and death. This is close to saying that ritual was the heart of a morality that distinguished men from beasts. This is also not far from the later Neo-Confucian synthesis, with its heavy stress on ritual, to be discussed shortly. Before doing that, however, it is advisable to explain the meaning of Neo-Confucianism.

Scholars agree that there is sufficient difference between the Confucianism of the *Analects* and the later version known as Neo-Confucianism to justify a new term. They also agree that there are sufficient similarities within Neo-Confucianism to take for granted the use of this term for a very long period of time. The beginning is difficult for a nonspecialist to ascertain exactly, but appears to have taken place before the time of famous reformer Wang An-shi, who died in 1086. The end came in 1912 with the final collapse of the Ch'ing dynasty. There is also general agreement that under Neo-Confucianism there was a noticeable tendency for the throne to become stronger in ways that created severe stress on the lives of the scholar-officials. Fascinating though this history is, our problem does not permit more than an occasional glance at it.

Two famous philosophers of the Neo-Confucian revival, Chu Hsi and Wang Yang-ming, present ideas relevant to this inquiry. Chu Hsi (1130–1200) is perhaps the more famous, on account of his synthesis of Sung Confucianism. The extracts from this synthesis in *Chinese Tradition* (1:479–502) have much to say about morality in general but do not appear to combine it with any conception of purity. On the other hand Chu Hsi is the compiler of a liturgy or ceremonial guide called *Family Rituals*,[38] which along with other sources provides unique glimpses of the working morality and recurring problems among what we may call the Chinese patriciate, not all of whom were active officials.

These rituals were a religiously saturated etiquette for the management of a patriarchal household. Hence the principal issues included the correct forms of ancestor worship, duties of children (especially sons to parents), and the proper way to introduce a bride into a patriarchal household.

There was in Neo-Confucianism a great deal of punctilious fussiness about ancient texts and the exact way to carry out rituals.[39] In the report of this fussiness I detected no signs of fear about pollution. Nor do the sources apparently have anything specific to say about what can happen if the ritual is not followed correctly. However, ordinary people were expected to become disorderly if rituals are neglected.[40] Like so much else in Confucianism, rites were expected to be edifying. Educated people who knew the proper way to perform rites were expected to change the customary practices of ordinary people in order to eliminate heterodoxy, a recurring aspect of popular revolts.[41] It is highly unlikely that this policy was at all effective.

Purity came into play only insofar as it was necessary to execute the rituals correctly, in accord with literary tradition. In this connection it is important to recall that family rituals were the closest practice to religious exercises available to China's Confucian upper stratum. They were what identified these people as real Chinese.[42] Nevertheless, there were two loopholes that permitted a slight degree of modification to suit new circumstances. In the first place the textual tradition was not free of ambiguities, a fact that required much scholarly interpretation. More significantly the basis of ritual was *li*, translated by Ebrey as ritual, manners, propriety. Li required adherence to forms. But Li in turn was man-made and therefore alterable.[43] This strictly human sanction for ritual contrasts sharply with the divine sanction found in the three monotheistic religions of the West and Near East. It is one important reason for the near absence of a militant moral purity in classical Confucianism.

In Chinese literature there is one well-documented tale of moral purity in opposition to authority. Though the tale is only marginally Confucian, we may mention it here because Chu Hsi

CHAPTER 4

was one of the later commentators who sanitized the story to make it more palatable for the Neo-Confucianists. He seems to have played an important role in its survival and distribution.

Ch'ü Yüan (338–278 B.C.)[44] lived almost exactly two centuries after Confucius (551–479 B.C.). Unlike Confucius he became one of the highest officials in the royal court of the kingdom of Ch'u. This was the age of Warring States (403–221 B.C.) before China's first and temporary unification. It was an age of dog-eat-dog competition, as each kingdom tried to win out over the others. Internally, and especially in the state of Ch'u, the competition between states was reflected in vicious struggles among cliques attempting to push the king towards different alliances and domestic policies. By no means all of these contests, it seems, were over distinct goals and policies. Much of the infighting appears to have been over pelf and prestige. Ch'ü Yüan started out as a trusted and talented minister of his king, but became trapped in this political morass. His enemies had him removed from the court and then banished. Out of loyalty to king and country, and confident of his own morality and the correctness of his ideas, he tried to remonstrate with the court and express his uncompromising ideals publicly. He showed his loyalty by refusing to flee to another country and seek office there, a common practice then. Finally his king was duped and murdered, and the state of Ch'u invaded and annexed. These events were too much for Ch'ü Yüan to bear. He drowned himself in the Milo River.

The essential tragedy that emerges from this account is one of loyalty unrequited by the sovereign, a loyalty based on inflexible moral principles. In what is widely regarded as a suicide note, Ch'ü Yüan left behind a long poem stating his case and justifying his choice of suicide. This poem, *Li Sao* (Encountering Sorrow), forms a major part of the legend of morally justified opposition that grew out of the fate of Ch'ü Yüan. Since, as Schneider shows so well, a great many other themes, from a defense of hermit dropouts to a call for a Chinese strong man, have attached themselves to Ch'ü Yüan's legend, it will be useful to examine *Li Sao* directly as one of our rare primary sources.[45]

124

In a first reading of *Li Sao* a Westerner could easily conclude that there is precious little in this ancient poem about moral purity and a great deal about moral superiority, verging on arrogance, and self-pity. Even more striking is the highly erotic language and imagery of the distressed official, presumably Ch'ü Yüan in his search for the king whose favor he had lost.[46] These lines suggest that in predynastic China loyalty to a superior could have a strong erotic component. Since *Li Sao* as a whole is a tragedy based on unrequited loyalty, the erotic aspect could be very significant.

On closer examination with the help of notes and commentaries, the reader finds several explicit claims to the author's purity. Thus the note on stanza 17, lines 67–70, asserts: "The drinking of dew and the eating of flowers indicate extreme purity. The dew represents the partisans of the good and pure with whom Ch'ü Yüan desires to associate." Further, on line 69 the commentary claims: "He emphasizes his own purity and sweetness by what he partakes of. His abhorrence of anything impure or ugly reveals the true character of the man."[47] In the text itself lines 117–118 present the image of a lonely hero standing his moral ground against all opponents:

> Men know me not. Let it be, even so!
> Indeed my feelings are quite true and pure.

Now just what does purity mean in this context? More exactly, what kinds of behavior does it exclude as impure? Taking the poem as a whole, the answer appears straightforward, though not free from contradictions. It excludes opportunism in giving advice to one's sovereign merely to please his whims, in a word, sycophancy. The advice should be both moral (in the sense of just and fair to all concerned) *and* politically effective. It is not always possible to combine these requirements, a point not discussed in the poem. Finally, one should remain loyal to one's sovereign in his time of troubles, even if the sovereign has been unjust, and in the end choose death over abandoning one's principles.

Thus *Li Sao* is a tragedy about the eternal conflict between moral principles—moral purity, if one prefers—and political expediency. It is no wonder that the tale appealed to disappointed scholar-officials throughout the long life of Dynastic China. What, if any, were the consequences? The answer, there too, is tragic. Like other "liberal" features of the Mandarinate's tradition, this moral current simply ran out into the sand without perceptible influence on the workings of governmental machinery. No doubt there are many reasons for the failure of the critical tradition within the ranks of scholarly officialdom.[48] The most important reason may be the absence in China of any social base for criticism outside the imperial administration, a situation very different from that in western Europe from the eighteenth century onwards. There was no independent nobility, no separate priesthood, no separate urban economy, thus no alternative ladders of status and prestige. A critical scholar-official, if he was lucky enough to avoid being beheaded, had only the choices of retirement or exile. Again, if he was lucky enough to have material resources such as family or clan land, he could live in exile or retirement, a life of comfort and cultivated futility. It was a very humane form of political death, and also very effective.

We may return now to the Neo-Confucian revival. The other philosopher that concerns us is Wang Yang-ming (1472–1529). Less well known than Chu Hsi, he flourished some three centuries later. He interests us because his writings present an argument that, without undue exegesis or other forms of intellectual tugging and hauling, begins to look like a theory of moral purity. All Confucians are of course theorists of morality ad nauseam. But a theory of moral purity?[49] Wang discusses the "activity of the mind in its natural purity and perfection," as the introduction puts it. In his own words, "Such a mind is rooted in [man's] Heaven-endowed nature, and is naturally intelligent, clear and not obscured. For this reason it is called the 'clear character.'"[50] The word "purity" does not occur in this specific sentence. But the term translated as "clear character" apparently carries overtones of purity in the sense of freedom from intellectual trash and nonsense, as well as from fantasies about prohibited behavior. As part of his very optimistic view of human nature, Wang Yang-ming further asserts, "The nature endowed in us by Heaven is pure and perfect." In other words he is saying that moral purity is somehow innate to human beings—a fallacy that is not unique to Western cultures. It is a strong current in Chinese thought ever since Mencius (ca. 371–ca. 289 B.C.).[51] At this point Wang faces the age-old problem of explaining the prevalence of immorality and evil in a world ruled at least intermittently by Heaven. Not surprisingly he puts the blame on "later generations." Supposedly they have been developing individualist notions that obscure the difference between right and wrong. The mind of man therefore becomes "concerned with fragmentary and isolated details, the desires of man become rampant [a frequent expression for uncontrolled behavior with sexual overtones] and the principle of Heaven is at an end."[52] It is, of course, necessary to avoid making too much of this striking similarity between the observations of a sixteenth-century Chinese philosopher and the widespread criticisms of moral decay in our own "advanced" societies. Nevertheless, such a parallel hints at the possibility that moral decay—or moral impurity—can display some similar aspects visible across a huge range of time and place. However that may be, Wang Yang-ming's remedy for evil is to teach people "to do good and remove evil in their will and thoughts." When that happens, "the impurities of the mind" will disappear.[53] Here the conception of moral impurities as something in the human mind becomes quite explicit. That this conception of moral purity remains worlds away from what we find in the Old Testament, the Huguenot, the Catholic, and the secular version displayed by the French Revolutionary radicals is obvious, to say the least. Missing or very weakly developed in China are the two basic themes in the Western theory and practice of moral purity. First is the otherworldly sanction for "our" moral purity, be it God, revolutionary faith, or the mythic Aryan race. The "will of heaven" lacks the power to bring about the fundamental changes in human affairs so widely attributed to Western notions. Second is a strongly developed notion of pollution that makes the impure and the unbelievers into a mysterious dehumanized threat that must, if at all possible, be rooted out for the sake of preserving "our" moral purity in our society, imperfect though that may be. These impure ones, especially in the form of the insufficiently faithful, are the main victims of bloody persecutions, from the guillotine radicalism of the French Revolution to the Stalinist purges and concentration camps, as well as in other cases discussed and not discussed here. Placing Western forms of moral purity in their historical development squarely alongside the record of Confucianism in China makes clear the relative feebleness of moral purity in Confucian thought and behavior. Confucianism never developed a sturdy theory and practice of persecution based on a theory of moral purity.

Conclusion

Perhaps the main finding of this book, at least the one that most surprised its author, has been that the theory and practice of moral purity was limited to the three monotheistic religions, Judaism, Christianity, and Islam. As we have just seen, the main Asiatic religions, Hinduism, Buddhism, and Confucianism, prior to the coming of the West showed only partial beginnings of persecuting movements for moral purity. Yet, as the meteoric rise of Maoism demonstrates, the decay of an Asian system of belief and social order has provided fertile soil for the most cruel versions of a search for moral purity. Even Hinduism, the most unlikely place for such a movement to take hold, has done all too well in producing these horrors. If we can no longer believe nineteenth-century theses about historical progress, we can easily see historical convergence in the causes of human suffering. Contrary to the banal prediction that East and West would never meet, they have joined to produce some of the twentieth century's worst misery.

✳ *Epilogue* ✳

IN CONCLUDING this book on moral purity, it is useful to do two things. One is to present some very brief observations on morality in general in order to do away with possible misapprehensions. The other is to pull together the arguments in this book by an abbreviated review of the main steps in its construction.

This book has not been intended as an attack on morality as such. Every human society, large and small, has a set of moral rules about what must be done and, more importantly, what must not be done. Moral rules are absolutely necessary to enable human beings to work and live together. Rules against murder and theft are familiar examples. By no means every rule in every society contributes to human welfare. Many do just the opposite: think of the rule about burning widows in Hindu India. But we cannot exist without morality.

This book has not been intended as an attack on moral purity, either. There is a sense in which moral purity is unavoidable. Any society that tried to adopt every moral rule suggested by anybody and everybody, native or foreign, would soon disintegrate into chaos. A certain amount of pride in the morality of one's own group is not necessarily offensive. Moral purity becomes dangerous only as it becomes the basis for persecution at home and abroad.

To recap, our tale began with a unique historical event, the invention of monotheism by the ancient Hebrews. It is well to at least mention the existence of other important Hebrew moral creations, such as the rendering of justice independently of the accused's status. Surrounded by polytheistic societies and facing widespread reluctance among their own followers—recall the objections to the taste of manna and the hankering after the fleshpots of Egypt—the advocates of monotheism had to be stern, convinced of their righteousness, and, on occasion, cruel. Such was the legacy of the ancient Hebrews to Christianity and Islam. Any doctrine that seeks to control all or nearly all of

129

human life sooner or later secretes heresies that are perceived as a moral and mortal threat. In the episode of the golden calf there was a threat even for early Judaism, which was not a proselytizing religion. Christianity and Islam were conquering faiths and very soon infested with heresies. In a monotheism threatened with splits, the founders' cruel discipline that created and sustained their religion's distinctive identity becomes the weapon against the heretics' challenge to that identity.

Many, though not all, of the cruel consequences of monotheism appear already in the Old Testament. However, an air of legend, with both possible exaggeration and concealment, hovers over these texts, despite the undoubted historicity of several. Therefore, to display and explain monotheism's consequences clearly it seemed wise to choose events from a later historical period. Histories of the papacy and of anti-Semitism presented a huge range of choices. The Massacre of St. Bartholomew, a critical event in the French Wars of Religion, came to mind as probably the worst slaughter of noncombatants in premodern times. The slaughter showed the vicious hostility of the Parisian populace toward the Huguenots. Permission and encouragement from the king were sufficient to set the rivers of blood flowing. But authorized aggression did not stop at religious hostilities. There was an element of poor against rich. The Huguenots, especially the flower of the movement at that moment gathered in Paris, were ostentatiously wealthy. Quite rapidly however, unfocused anger and cupidity ceased to have specific targets, religious or secular. Catholics murdered and plundered Catholics. Even children killed other children. This evidence raises the possibility that in France at that time religious conflict with the horrors of persecution, mainly an affair of the literate, was not the main source of popular anger and cruelty. Other grievances and sentiments—such as poor against rich, rage at extortion by tax collectors and landlords, an erratic supply of food, anger at the incomprehensible behavior of markets, and, finally, an increase in sheer human nastiness created by all these and other factors—may have been more important than doctrinal quarrels. These hostile feelings could attach themselves indiscriminately to Catholic or Huguenot organizations as the most obvious targets for the expression of assorted feelings of outrage.

In the French Wars of Religion *two* monotheisms—or two competing variants of one—by force of circumstances evolved into stern religious movements, each with authoritarian self-discipline, each convinced of their God-given righteousness, and each very cruel. From all this it becomes clear that heresy brings out the most vicious aspects of monotheism.

The French Revolution showed for the first time in history that enormous cruelty can exist without religious monotheism yet with intense concern about moral purity. In monotheism's place we find the moral justification for slaughter in the concept of revolutionary purity. Purity from sin and temptation had long been part of the heretic mentality and even to some extent of orthodox Catholic Christianity. Revolutionary purity promised to bring about the morally pure, petit-bourgeois utopia.

This emphasis on revolutionary purity can be traced to the circumstances of the time. Like all moral movements, purist radicalism had specific historical causes. As usual, the moderates had not been able to cope with the problems thrown up by the Revolution's success in overthrowing the monarchy and much of the rest of the Old Regime. The moderates' failures gave the radical purists their opportunity. The radicals did solve the major problem of the Revolution's survival. But they guillotined so many of their own followers for the sake of revolutionary purity that they lost the support of their own followers, who turned on Robespierre, Saint-Just, and others, ending the radical revolution. Purity then became something for "other people" to consider.

To avoid the illusion of inevitability, we must again briefly review the human struggles that brought about the events just mentioned. By about the 1790s the Revolution's leaders faced enemies on the frontiers, corruption, inefficiency, treachery, and counterrevolution in broad areas of France. The response that produced revolutionary victory over these obstacles was the

Committee of Public Safety (established April 6, 1793). This revolutionary autocracy greatly improved the flow of manpower and supplies to the French armies and ended the threat of a counterrevolutionary victory at home. There is a tendency to downplay these achievements, partly on account of hostility toward the revolutionary enterprise as a whole, partly on account of the role of the terror. Indeed, terror increased as the Revolution became more secure. Towards the end of this reign of revolutionary terror, the guillotine became explicitly an educational device for helping to create a new and pure revolutionary humanity.

It is at this historical juncture, when the notion had become completely secular, that the idea of moral purity became most ominous. Revolutionary purity was one of the most powerful legacies of the French Revolution—to Stalinism, Maoism, and even Nazism. With this legacy our soundings of moral purity in Western contexts came to an end.

Turning to Asia, our last chapter surveyed Hinduism, Buddhism, and Confucianism to discover what these religions display in the way of a conception of moral purity. Our study showed that, as a society based on gradations of purity-impurity, Hindu India provides a striking contrast with the West and that outside of monotheism there can be pollution without persecution. But the price turned out to be heavy in India's rigid hierarchy of caste. Polluters were far from accepted members of Hindu society. Furthermore, in recent years Hindu Nationalists have had striking success in catching up with the worst features of Western persecution on behalf of purity. The same is true of China, where in an earlier period Confucianism narrowly escaped from turning into a persecuting state doctrine. With the intrusion of the West and the victory of Mao, this changeover happened with a vengeance. Mao's attempt to enforce revolutionary purity through the Cultural Revolution was a cruel and unmitigated disaster. Buddhism, generally a nonpersecuting doctrine, is now for the most part confined to remote corners of the world such as Tibet, where it is manifestly the victim of persecution, not its promoter.

Thus a central conclusion of this study, that militant, organized persecution was a product of monotheism and largely absent in Asia, offers no grounds for hope. Asian societies now offer no refuge for romantic escapism. More generally, with the collapse of the Soviet Union, long a major bastion for a relentless doctrinal purity, indigenous variants of demands for moral purity have sprouted up all over the world, from the United States to the continent of India.

Not so long ago, say, shortly after the Second World War, it seemed that the battles against the most virulent forms of irrationality and intolerance were over and won. We could turn to the struggle against ignorance, disease, and hunger, and perhaps even enjoy life a bit. A half century later, that whole outlook looks, with the return of all the old ghosts and the creation of new horrors, like the great illusion of the twentieth century.

* *Notes* *

CHAPTER 1
MORAL PURITY AND IMPURITY IN THE OLD TESTAMENT

1. On this score see Edward Westermarck, *The Origin and Develop-ment of the Moral Ideas,* 2d ed., vol. 2 (London, 1917), index, s.v. "Pollution"; and William Graham Sumner and Albert Galloway Keller, *The Science of Society,* vol. 4 (New Haven, 1927), index, s.v. "Uncleanness." Both works are treasures of worldwide ethnographic and historical data to be used with critical caution.

2. According to Lev. 20:10 the penalty for adultery was death for both partners.

3. The prohibition against homosexuality also occurs at Lev. 20:13 and that against bestiality at Lev. 20:15–16. The latter passages, how-ever, do not give any evaluation of this behavior.

4. See the works of Sumner and Keller, and Westermarck, cited above.

5. Mary Douglas, *Purity and Danger: An Analysis of the Concepts of Pol-lution and Taboo* (London, 1994).

6. Jacob Milgrom, *Leviticus 1–16: A New Translation with Introduction and Commentary* (New York, 1991), 42–43; hereafter referred to in the text as *Leviticus 1–16.*

7. A problem of translation arises here. The King James Version uses the expression trespass offering here and at 5:15. The Revised Standard Version speaks of a guilt offering at 5:6 and breach of faith at 5:15, both instead of trespass. Milgrom uses the expression sacrilege in several passages instead of trespass (see Milgrom, *Leviticus 1–16,* 319–330, 345–356). Sacrilege has the advantage of emphasizing that certain acts were regarded as assaults on holy areas or objects and therefore utterly immoral. Presumably trespass conveyed this notion adequately in the seventeenth century, as indicated by the entry in the *Oxford Universal Dictionary.* It is appropriate to add here that our interest in the cor-rectness of any translation is distinctly minor. We are interested in the King James Version of the Bible as a source of specific moral notions. Mistranslations in it have been part of our Western heritage for four centuries.

8. Lev. 22 entire; Milgrom (*Leviticus 1–16*, 46) states that the opposite to holiness is impurity. But see the diagram on p. 732 where Milgrom makes "common" the opposite of "holy."

9. Milgrom, *Leviticus 1–16*, 686–687.

10. See Mary Douglas, *Purity and Danger*, chap. 3, for a history of the debates and her claim that the concept of holiness constitutes a governing principle.

11. Westermarck (*Development of Moral Ideas*, 2:290–345) provides an exhaustive survey of dietary restrictions. For a more immediately relevant example see Milgrom's exhaustive and very interesting discussion of the Hebrew's rejection of the pig as a source of food in *Leviticus 1–16*, 649–653. Avoidance of pigs was widespread in the ancient Near East, partly because they were seen as filthy and religiously contaminating, partly on account of the connection with chthonic deities who competed with monotheism. However, the refusal to eat its flesh did not become a test of the Jews' loyalty to Judaism until Hellenistic times (p. 652). Thus what one won't eat becomes a symbol of social identity. Could that be the reason why subadolescent girls nowadays often go through a phase of being very finicky about food? Refusal to eat is a standard gesture of opposition to authority.

12. Milgrom (*Leviticus 1–16*, 1002) connects bodily impurities with death [obviously wrong in the case of feces, ignored by the Bible] and asserts that "the eternal struggle between the forces of good and evil, life and death—removed by Israel from the polytheistic theomachy to the inner life of man"—is represented in the scriptural accounts of pollution. To my way of thinking, Milgrom's thesis here requires undue ingenuity in the service of an edifying conclusion. The facts of a helter-skelter moral code don't fit the conclusion that neatly. Nevertheless, his stress on the moral consequences of the change from polytheism to monotheism is very fruitful.

13. Milgrom (*Leviticus 1–16*, 821–823) stresses the origin of scale disease in divine wrath and its resulting moral aspect, which came into full flower in rabbinic literature.

14. David's ordering the death of Uriah the Hittite so that he might take Uriah's wife is not described as immoral. Instead, David's action was "sin that displeased the Lord" and for which he would be severely punished. See 2 Sam. 11:27, 12:13. According to the third revised edition of the *Oxford Universal Dictionary* (1955), the word "moral," mean-

ing concerned about vice and virtue and rules of right conduct, does not appear until late Middle English, which would put it in the fourteenth century. However, there are obvious moral concerns in Western languages much closer to Hebrew in time. Greek tragedy is full of such concerns and has generated a large literature about them.

Chapter 2
Purity in the Religious Conflicts of Sixteenth-Century France

1. Pierre Imbart de la Tour, *Les origines de la réforme* (Geneva, 1978), 3:158–161, 163, 169.
2. Imbart de la Tour, *Origines,* 3:324–327, 343.
3. Ibid., 3:65–66.
4. J. Michelet, *Histoire de France,* rev. ed. (Paris, 1856), 2:74–75. Modern scholarship confirms the absence of any militant plebeian Calvinism through the 1530s. Henry Heller (*Iron and Blood: Civil Wars in Sixteenth-Century France* [Montreal, 1991], 45) places the conjuncture of religious nonconformity with popular protest in the 1540s. Wayne te Brake (*Shaping History: Ordinary People in European Politics* [Berkeley and Los Angeles, 1998], 64) reports the first clandestine Calvinist meeting to organize a revolutionary church in May 1559.
5. Michelet, *Histoire de France,* 2:77, 80–81.
6. Ibid., 2:86.
7. Joseph Lecler, S. J., *Toleration and the Reformation,* trans. T. L. Westow (New York, 1960), 2:10.
8. Aubrey Galpern, *Religions of the People in Sixteenth-Century Champagne* (Cambridge, Mass., 1976), 16–20; quotation from p. 20.
9. Galpern, *Religions of the People,* 43.
10. Ibid., 48, 53–54.
11. Ibid., 122.
12. Ibid., 123.
13. Ibid., 167.
14. Jean Calvin, *L'Institution Chrétienne* (Editions Kerygma, 1978), bk. 2, ch. 8, sec. 41, 43.
15. Calvin, *L'Institution Chrétienne,* bk. 1, ch. 15, sec. 8.
16. Ibid., sec. 1.
17. Ibid., sec. 8.
18. For the Calvinist virtues see Calvin, *L'Institution Chrétienne,* bk. 1, ch. 17, sec. 2, final paragraph; bk. 2, ch. 8, sec. 6 (lists of behaviors to

be avoided and demands pure thought); bk. 3, ch. 10, sec. 1 (advocates temperance in the use of God's material gifts, rejects rigorism); bk. 4, ch. 1, sec. 13B (similar to preceding but with more sarcasm).

19. Ibid., bk. 3, ch. 22, sec. 1, end. See also bk. 3, ch. 1, sec. 1 for God's threat of death eternal with lightning playing about our heads.

20. Ibid., bk. 3, ch. 21, sec. 7.

21. Ernest Lavisse, ed., *Histoire de France,* vol. 6, pt. 1 (1559–1598) by J. H. Mariéjol (Paris, 1911), 34–35. Despite its age Lavisse (more precisely Mariéjol) is an excellent source for the high politics and major religious controversies from 1559 to the Edict of Nantes in 1598. Though detailed, the narrative is clear, with many quotations from original sources.

22. Lecler, *Toleration and the Reformation,* 2:47 n. 2. Emphasis added.

23. For a penetrating analysis that sheds valuable light on the general role of kingship, see David Teasley, "The Charge of Sodomy as a Political Weapon in Early Modern France: The Case of Henry III in the Catholic League Polemic 1585–1589," *Maryland Historian* 18, no. 1 (Spring/Summer 1987), 17–30.

24. Lavisse, *Histoire de France,* vol. 6, pt. 1, 34–35.

25. Ibid., 47–49.

26. For details, see Joseph Lecler, *Toleration and the Reformation* 2:40–121.

27. J. B. Bury (*A History of Freedom of Thought,* 2d ed. [Oxford, 1952], 56) quotes the remark without giving a citation. It is not given in *Bartlett's Familiar Quotations* (15th ed., 1980), nor does it occur in Henry Kamen, *The Rise of Toleration* (London, 1967). I could not find it in Montaigne's *Essays.* It may well be apocryphal. Whatever its source, the remark was crisply on target, and not only for the sixteenth century.

28. On the fusing of Huguenot complaints with the economic anxieties and angers of the poorer town and city dwellers, see the excellent study by Henry Heller, *The Conquest of Poverty: The Calvinist Revolt in Sixteenth-Century France* (Leiden, 1986). From this account it also appears that Calvin's ideas about obedience to unjust authority made a major contribution to stamping out the flames of popular insurrection.

29. For Calvin's Geneva, see E. William Monter, *Enforcing Morality in Early Modern Europe* (London, 1987) articles 2 and 3. This is a collection of articles originally published between 1966 and 1986.

30. Henri-Leonard Bordier, *Le Chansonnier Huguenot du XVIe siècle* (Geneva, 1969). Songs cited by number and by date, where given. The series begins on p. 97.

31. Anyone curious about the age and tenacity of clerical practices deemed serious abuses would do well to consult Henry C. Lea, *The History of Sacerdotal Celibacy in the Christian Church* (New York, 1957; originally published Philadelphia, 1866), especially chap. 21, "Results" (of efforts to impose celibacy from the thirteenth to fifteenth centuries), and chap. 24, "The Fifteenth Century" (recording sacerdotal demoralization at that time). Equally valuable is Henry C. Lea, *A History of Auricular Confession and Indulgences in the Latin Church,* vol. 3 (New York, 1968; copyrighted by Lea, 1896), chaps. 1, 2, 3, 5 on indulgences. No modern scholar would be likely to draw a simple casual connection between clerical abuses, which had been going on for centuries, and the Reformation that began in the sixteenth century. Nevertheless, just why some ancient abuses rather suddenly seemed intolerable to some people remains a crucial historical problem. The Marxist answer to the effect that people find an abuse intolerable as soon as they discover it is possible to do something about it is in my estimation not very helpful. Was it really easier to correct clerical abuses after 1500? The results hardly support such a view. Did large numbers of people really get much more excited about them after 1500? If so, why? In the late sixteenth century "outside agitators" obviously made a big contribution to setting the tumult in motion. Under what conditions do such individuals appear and succeed, at least for a time? If persuasive answers to these questions exist, I should like to learn about them.

32. Lavisse, *Histoire de France,* vol. 6, pt. 1, 95. See also pp. 124–125 for her decision to have Coligny murdered. Her role has been the subject of debate through the centuries.

33. Philippe Erlanger, *St. Bartholomew's Night,* trans. Patrick O'Brian (New York, 1962), 144–156.

34. Sylvia Lennis England, *The Massacre of St. Bartholomew* (London, 1938), 127. See also Erlanger, *St. Bartholomew's Night,* 144, 176–177, 242.

35. Erlanger, *St. Bartholomew's Night,* 168.

36. Lavisse, *Histoire de France,* vol. 6, pt. 1, 132–133.

37. Michelet, *Histoire de France,* 12:6. The first chapter in this volume, pp. 1–13, discusses the immediate reaction to the Massacre. Michelet's thesis holds that politics took charge at once. About this one may ask: When, if ever, have political considerations not been paramount?

38. Donald R. Kelley, "Martyrs, Myths and the Massacre: The Background of St. Bartholomew," in *The Massacre of St. Bartholomew: Reappraisals and Documents,* ed. Alfred Soman (The Hague, 1974), 199.

39. Natalie Zemon Davis, "The Rites of Religious Violence in Sixteenth-Century France," in *The Massacre of St. Bartholomew: Reappraisals and Documents,* ed. Alfred Soman (The Hague, 1974), 209–210.

40. Davis, "Religious Violence," 211.

41. Ibid., 218. On p. 230 Davis criticizes the thesis that religious riots were actually cases of the "people" attacking the rich, using the argument that figures show the victims of the riots to be artisans, "little people" in large numbers. Agreeing heartily with Davis's emphasis on pollution in the religious themes in the riots, I nevertheless find this argument unconvincing. Heller, writing much later, has documented the struggle between rich and poor in many parts of France. When the poor lose out, as they often did, this fact will swell the number of little people among the victims. More generally, little people, so far as I can make out, formed the bulk of the rioters on *both* Catholic and Protestant sides. Naturally, therefore, most of the casualties will be little people. Nowadays we can see that beneath and alongside the religious conflict there was one between rich and poor that from time to time flamed out into the open.

42. Emmanuel Le Roy Ladurie, *Carnival in Romans,* trans. Mary Feeney (New York, 1979), xiv.

43. Le Roy Ladurie, *Carnival,* 19; for a more detailed account of alignments and grievances, see 138–145.

44. Ibid., 16, 17, on the poor.

45. Ibid., 80.

46. Ibid., 188, 237.

47. Ibid., 218–227.

48. Ibid., 249.

49. Ibid., 257, 258, 261–262.

50. Kelly, "Martyrs," 198.

51. Daniel Jonah Goldhagen, *Hitler's Willing Executioners: Ordinary Germans and the Holocaust* (New York, 1996); on dehumanization, 398; gratuitous brutality, 228, 236–237; picnic atmosphere with snapshot mementos, 246–247. On p. 407 there is a snapshot of a German soldier taking aim at a Jewish mother and child during a major slaughter of the Jews in the Ukraine in 1942. It is highly unlikely that such an event was unique. With the possible exception of this picture, the material cited above describes the behavior of the notorious Police Battalion 101. This battalion was made up of "ordinary Germans" in the sense that it was a rough cross-section of German males, and def-

initely not a collection of fanatic Nazis. Its task was to exterminate Jews in Russia in 1942. To my knowledge no one has challenged a single fact in Goldhagen's account of this battalion, the most sensational part of his book, nor any other of the mass of facts in the rest of the book. Goldhagen's thesis that Hitler's executioners included a large number of willing, ordinary Germans strikes me as irrefutable. Whether the rest of Germany's ordinary Germans were like those in Police Battalion 101 is another question, and one for which no definite answer may be possible. Goldhagen's account of widespread and pervasive German anti-Semitism points in that direction. But that is hardly the end of the matter.

CHAPTER 3

PURITY AS A REVOLUTIONARY CONCEPT IN THE FRENCH REVOLUTION

1. Le Robert, *Dictionnaire Historique de la Langue Française,* new ed. (1993, 2:1671), s.v. "Pur."

2. J. J. Rousseau, "Discours si le Réstablissement des Sciences et des Arts A Contribué à Épurer les Moeurs," in Henri Guillermin, *Du Contrat Social* (Paris, 1963), 199–232. The question in the title was set for a "concours d'éloquence" in 1749. Rousseau won the prize, for which he claimed no gratification since it failed to advance his career in 1750.

3. See the excellent discussion of primitivism in Peter Gay, *The Enlightenment, an Interpretation: The Science of Freedom* (New York, 1969), 93–96.

4. For an unsurpassed study of the erosion of legitimacy in the Old Regime, manifested in the writings of famous and obscure thinkers, see Daniel Mornet, *Les Origines intellectuelles de la révolution française 1715–1787,* 6th ed. (Paris, 1967); originally published 1933. Mornet emphasizes the role of secularization. Evidently what happened to the concept of purity was part of a much larger trend.

5. François Furet and Mona Ozouf, *La Gironde et les Girondins* (Paris, 1991); and Albert Soboul, ed., *Actes du Colloque Girondins et Montognards* (Paris, 1980).

6. Jacques-Pierre Brissot de Warville, *Mémoires* (Paris, 1877).

7. Brissot, *Mémoires,* 220.

8. Ibid. 427–428. A constitution granting equal rights to all would, Brissot claimed, cure these evils. Hardly anyone had feasible remedies for France's ills.

141

9. It was imperative to prove that defeated revolutionaries were immoral during their brief appearance on the revolutionary stage. The Girondins were clearly moderates—and condemned as such by their opponents—according to the shifting political spectrum of the day. But that does not mean that they had a principled objection to revolutionary violence. The Gironde's newspapers supported or condoned the worst outbreak of popular violence against mainly innocent victims, the September Massacres, September 2–7, 1792. See Marcel Dorigny, "Violence et Révolution: les Girondins et les Massacres de Septembre," in Soboul, *Girondins et Montagnards,* 103–120.

10. For the main points in the controversy see A. Aulard, *Danton,* 12th ed. (Paris, 1903). This is a textbook presentation of the hero of the Revolution by *the* authority at the turn of the century. It contains a useful collection of Danton's speeches. A. Mathiez, *Autour de Danton* (Paris, 1926) is the angry reaction of a young scholar holding a provincial post, professor at the University of Dijon, resenting Aulard's fame and access to archives available only in Paris. Along with the venom there are straightforward factual assertions in Mathiez's book that destroy the heroic image of Danton.

11. Aulard, *Danton,* 84.

12. Ibid., 103–104.

13. See below his contemptuous and obscene remarks on revolutionary ideals that he made to Robespierre.

14. Louis Jacob, *Hébert le Père Duchesne: chef des sans-culottes* (Paris, 1960), 128. This source is useful on account of its numerous and full quotations.

15. Jacob, *Hébert,* 37.

16. Ibid., 212–213.

17. Ibid., 234. However, previous pages show Hébert to have been far from an out and out supporter of dechristianization.

18. Ibid., 325. See p. 343 for a similar remark on the purity of the Commune. Neither remark is by Hébert.

19. Ibid., 259.

20. Ibid., 297. Unlike many writers of the time, Hébert had no interest in the general concept of a free man. Here he merely wanted to assert that money-mad traders did not deserve to be citizens.

21. This and the other themes recur so frequently in Jacob's extensive quotations of *Père Duchesne* as to make specific citation profuse, burdensome, and probably superfluous. Dishonesty and corruption,

in the sense of self-enrichment from public funds at the expense of revolutionary objectives, was likewise a major reason.

22. See Olivier Blanc, *La Corruption sous La Terreur 1792–1794* (Paris, 1992).

23. See Blanc, *La Corruption,* chap. 3, pp. 55–67, on this issue. It is far from clear that the British got anything for their money.

24. The *Oeuvres de Maximilien Robespierre* take up ten volumes. Fortunately volume 10, *Discours 27 Juillet 1793–27 Juillet 1794,* contains much of the material most useful for this inquiry. Because of the great bulk of the *Oeuvres* and their inaccessibility, in addition to volume 10 I have relied on the selection in the three-volume collection in *Les Classiques du peuple, Robespierre: Textes Choisis* (Paris, 1956–1958). Other special studies will be cited at appropriate points.

25. William Doyle, *The Oxford History of the French Revolution* (Oxford, 1989), 266.

26. Daniel P. Jordan, *The Revolutionary Career of Maximilien Robespierre* (New York, 1985), 141.

27. See his *Oeuvres,* 10:133–134. Jordan (*Robespierre,* 182) points out that Robespierre's first personal involvement in the terror came about in connection with the Girondins.

28. *Oeuvres,* 10:223.

29. See Albert Mathiez, *Études sur Robespierre* (Paris, 1988), 108–111; and Robespierre, "Sur les subsistances," December 2, 1792, in *Textes Choisis,* 2:82–90. Mathiez regards this speech as a step towards price control *(Maximum),* passed on September 17, 1793, and widely evaded. The editor of the *Textes Choisis* asserts on the other hand that this speech is the only text that reveals "with beautiful clarity the utopias from which perished the petty bourgeois dictatorship of the Jacobins" (p. 82).

30. Doyle, *French Revolution,* 437. The Maximum did not go into effect formally until September 29, 1793.

31. Robespierre, *Oeuvres,* 10:113–114.

32. For Robespierre's refusal to name those he denounced, saying only they were members of both committees (Committee of Public Safety and Committee of General Security), see the report of the Jacobin session of 8 Thermidor (July 26, 1794) in *Oeuvres,* 10:584.

33. For the final drama, see Doyle, *French Revolution,* 279–281.

34. Robespierre, "Sur les Principes de Morale Politique," February 17, 1794, *Textes Choisis,* 3:112–113.

35. Robespierre, "Le Procès du roi," December 3, 1792, *Textes Choisis,* 2:73.

36. Robespierre, "Sur les subsistances," December 2, 1792, *Textes Choisis,* 2:89.

37. Robespierre, "Sur le gouvernement représentatif," May 10, 1793, *Textes Choisis,* 2:145–146.

38. Robespierre, "Sur les Principes de Morale Politique," 3:118.

39. Robespierre, "Sur le gouvernement représentatif," 2:154.

40. Robespierre, "Sur les Principes de Morale Politique," 3:117–118.

41. Robespierre, "Sur le gouvernement représentatif," 2:142.

42. Robespierre, "Exposition de mes principes," May 1792, *Textes Choisis,* 1:160.

43. Robespierre, "Le Procès du roi," 2:75.

44. Robespierre, "Sur le gouvernement représentatif," 2:143.

45. Robespierre, "Sur les subsistances," 2:90.

46. Robespierre, *Textes Choisis,* 3:102–103.

47. Text in *Oeuvres,* 10:542–576.

48. The French victory in the battle of Fleurus, June 26, 1794, was a severe blow to the anti-French coalition. On the economy, see the remarks in Doyle, *French Revolution,* 264–265.

49. Robespierre, "Sur la conspiration tramée contre la liberté," April 10, 1793, *Textes Choisis,* 2:123.

50. Robespierre, "Sur les subsistances," 2:90.

51. Since the collected works of Saint-Just take up only one volume as against Robespierre's ten, references here will be mainly to Saint-Just, *Oeuvres Complètes,* édition établie par Michèle Duval (Paris, 1984). His incomplete and unpublished writings, also collected here, pp. 928–1009, are especially revealing about some of his hopes and fears. Saint-Just, *Discours et Rapports* (Paris, 1957) is mainly helpful in determining dates by the Gregorian calendar when a text in *Oeuvres Complètes* reports them only by the Revolutionary calendar. It also has brief notes on the political context of the speeches. But the best source for such information is the excellent and detailed biography: Jörg Monar, *Saint-Just: Sohn, Denker, und Protagonist Der Revolution* (Bonn, 1993).

52. Saint-Just, *Oeuvres Complètes,* 521.

53. Ibid., 527.

54. On the mission to the army of the Rhine, see Monar, *Saint-Just,* 447–487.

55. For the background of the speech, see Monar, *Saint-Just,* 422–434.

56. Saint-Just, *Oeuvres Complètes,* 520–521.

57. Ibid., 521.

58. Ibid., 522–523.

59. Ibid., 528–529.

60. Ibid., 530.

61. Ibid., 415–425.

62. Ibid., 301. The "Esprit" is very long, pp. 276–348 in this text. The date and form of publication, if indeed it was published, seem to be unknown. The *Oeuvres Complètes* gives no clue. Monar (*Saint-Just,* 193) gives the impression Saint-Just wrote it during the winter of 1790–1791.

63. Saint-Just, *Oeuvres Complètes,* 457–478.

64. Ibid., 477–478.

65. Ibid., 476.

66. Saint-Just, *Discours Et Rapports,* ed. Albert Soboul (Paris, 1957), 152–153n. For the complex situation at the time of Hébert's death, see Doyle, *French Revolution,* 271–275.

67. Doyle, *French Revolution,* 259–262, on dechristianization; see also 266–269, 276.

68. Saint-Just, *Oeuvres Complètes,* 699.

69. Ibid., 700.

70. Ibid., 706.

71. Ibid., 707.

72. Ibid., 722–738; and Doyle, *French Revolution,* 269–270, for essential background.

73. Saint-Just, *Oeuvres Complètes,* 723.

74. Ibid., 729.

75. Ibid., 731.

76. Ibid., 736.

77. Doyle, *French Revolution,* 269–270.

78. Saint-Just, *Oeuvres Complètes,* 760–779.

79. Report in the Name of the Committee of Public Safety and the Committee of General Security (on criminal factions aiming to absorb the Revolution into a change of dynasty and against Danton, Camille Desmoulins, and others) [title abbreviated by author]. Delivered before the National Convention, 11 Germinal, Year II (March 31, 1794), according to Monar, *Saint-Just,* 584. For the political maneuvering behind the decision to attack Danton, see Monar, pp. 580–584.

80. Ibid., 761.

81. Ibid., 770.

82. Ibid., 778.

83. Ibid., 806–822.

84. Ibid., 809.

85. Ibid., 811.

86. Danton seems to have been the only revolutionary leader who displayed utter contempt for the rhetoric of the utopian future, master though he was of other inspirational techniques. For a revealing outburst of contempt by Danton that contributed to his execution see Monar, *Saint-Just*, 583.

87. Saint-Just, *Oeuvres Complètes*, 812–813.

88. For a good modern discussion of Legalism, see Benjamin I. Schwartz, *The World of Thought in Ancient China* (Cambridge, Mass., 1985), chap. 8.

89. Saint-Just, *Oeuvres Complètes*, 820–822.

90. On the law and its effects, see Doyle, *French Revolution*, 275. Monar (*Saint-Just*, 686) gives statistics on the rise in death sentences.

91. Monar, *Saint-Just*, 679, 685.

92. Quoted again in Monar, *Saint-Just*, 689, from *Oeuvres Complètes*, 818, 820.

93. Monar, *Saint-Just*, 690, with quotations from and citations of Robespierre's speeches.

94. Ibid., 690–692.

95. Ibid., 692–694.

96. They occur among unfinished writings in "Fragments d'Institutions Républicaines," *Oeuvres Complètes*, 966–1009. For a discussion of the date of composition, see Monar, *Saint-Just*, 706–707.

97. Quoted with discussion in Monar, *Saint-Just*, 710; text in *Oeuvres Complètes*, 975–976.

98. Monar, *Saint-Just*, 710–711.

99. Saint-Just, *Oeuvres Complètes*, 979.

100. The history of religions shows that under favorable circumstances a small group of people can set off a movement that amounts to a huge moral transformation—if not a revolution and by no means what the founders sought—among enormous populations. On the other hand, by the close of the twentieth century it had become obvious that the revolutionary impulse had degenerated into corruption all over the globe. A partial response has been the return to religion, taking with it

one of the ugliest features of the revolutionary tradition: violence in behalf of dogmatic certainty about one's own brand of moral purity.

101. The tale of his last days is too dramatic to summarize without distortion. Monar presents a carefully constructed and moving account, based on numerous sources. See his *Saint-Just*, 679–704, 733–779.

102. Saint-Just, *Oeuvres Complètes*, 909.

103. Ibid., 917.

104. Monar, *Saint-Just*, 763–764. This fragment did not make its way into the *Oeuvres Complètes*.

105. Ibid., 763–764.

106. Ibid., 777–778.

107. V. O. Kliuchevskii, *Kurs Russkoi Istorii* (Moskva, 1958; originally published in the 1870s), Chast' 5, Lektsiya 87, 65–67.

108. For England, see F. M. L. Thompson, *The Rise of Respectable Society: A Social History of Victorian Britain* (Cambridge, Mass., 1988). The case of the Prussian bureaucracy in Wilhelmine Germany is more ambiguous. A remarkable article by Peter-Christian Witt, "Der Preussische Landrat als Steuerbeamter 1891–1918 . . ." (in I. Geiss and Bj. Wende, eds., *Deutschland in der Weltpolitik des 19 und 20 Jahrhunderts* [Düsseldorf, 1973], 205–219), uncovered widespread connivance by government officials with tax evasion by the Junkers. Nevertheless, there is no reason to doubt the widespread German pride in their efficient and fair bureaucracy, even if the pride was far from altogether justified. These major social and intellectual developments were invisible over the historical horizon for the French revolutionary radical leaders. If they had a glimpse of the future, as did Mao before the Cultural Revolution, would they have acted in the same destructive way? It seems that for Robespierre the answer would be yes and for Saint-Just possibly no. But, as a not so kindly veil hides the future, the iron wall of death and destruction hides many parts of the past.

CHAPTER 4
NOTES ON PURITY AND POLLUTION IN ASIATIC CIVILIZATIONS

1. Michael Moffatt, *An Untouchable Community in South India: Structure and Consensus* (Princeton, 1979), 27, after Dumont.

2. A. L. Basham, *The Wonder That Was India*, 1st Evergreen ed. (New York, 1959), 145.

3. Basham, *Wonder*, 145.

4. "Twice born" refers to natural birth followed by the second birth of initiation into Aryan society.

5. Basham, *Wonder,* 145.

6. L. S. S. O'Malley, *Popular Hinduism: The Religion of the Masses* (Cambridge, 1935), 79. For more details see *Encyclopaedia Brittannica,* 11th ed., s.v. "Thugs."

7. For a useful if somewhat pedestrian account, see Yogendra K. Malik and V. B. Singh, *Hindu Nationalists in India: The Rise of the Bharatiya Janata Party* (New Delhi, 1995).

8. There is a good account in Malik and Singh, *Hindu Nationalists,* 127–132.

9. William Theodore de Bary, ed., *Sources of Indian Tradition* (New York, 1958), 1:90. Cited hereafter as *Indian Tradition.*

10. *Indian Tradition,* 1:98–99.

11. For an official Buddhist description of Nirvana, complete with all the necessary contradictions, evasions, and confusions, see *Indian Tradition,* 1:103.

12. William Theodore de Bary et al., eds., *Sources of Chinese Tradition* (New York, 1960), 1:266, 270. Cited hereafter as *Chinese Tradition.*

13. *Chinese Tradition,* 1:270.

14. Ibid., 1:270–271.

15. Ibid., 1:271–272.

16. Ibid., 1:288–291.

17. Ibid., 1:272.

18. Ibid., 1:335–336.

19. Edward Conze, *Buddhist Texts Through the Ages* (Oxford, 1954), 202–206; and, on women, *Chinese Tradition,* 1:334–335.

20. Edward Conze, *Buddhist Wisdom Books* (London, 1958), 46–47.

21. *Chinese Tradition,* 1:336.

22. Ibid., 1:338–339.

23. *Indian Tradition,* 1:108.

24. Ibid., 1:161.

25. *Indian Tradition,* 1:98; *Chinese Tradition,* 1:266–267.

26. *Chinese Tradition,* 1:267–268; *Indian Tradition,* 1:102.

27. *Chinese Tradition,* 1:270.

28. *Indian Tradition,* 1:114–115.

29. Ibid., 1:118.

30. On Buddhism and war, see the meaty summary in Herbert Franke, "Mongol Rulers as Buddhist Universal Emperors." *Bayerische*

Akademie der Wissenschaften (Philosophisch-Historische Klasse, Sitzungs-berichte: Jahrgang 1978 Heft 2), 53–54. Franke remarks, inter alia, that Buddhism, "which forbade to kill living beings, could serve as legit-imizing ideology for a people of warriors like the Mongols." Religious beliefs are no bar to cruelty and violence, as the history of Christianity also demonstrates.

31. There is a good brief treatment of popular rebellions and their leadership, especially the White Lotus, in Wolfgang Bauer, *China and the Search for Happiness: Recurring Themes in Four Thousand Years of Chinese Cultural History*, trans. Michael Shaw (New York, 1976), 223–225.

32. John King Fairbank, *China: A New History* (Cambridge, Mass., 1992), 54–57, gives a brief, up-to-date account. In the modern translit-eration Ch'in becomes Qin.

33. Bauer, *Search for Happiness*, 206. See also Arthur F. Wright, *Buddhism in Chinese History* (Stanford, 1959), 83–85, for the circumstances that made the persecution possible, essentially the xenophobia of the declining T'ang dynasty.

34. Fairbank, *China*, 79.

35. Bauer, *Search for Happiness*, 206–207.

36. *The Analects of Confucius,* translated and annotated by Arthur Waley (New York, 1938), 16, 21, 23.

37. Bauer, *Search for Happiness*, 50; see also Patricia Buckley Ebrey, *Confucianism and Family Rituals in Imperial China: A Social History of Writing about Rites* (Princeton, 1991), chap. 2.

38. Ebrey, *Family Rituals,* 6. Chu Hsi's book is the core of this anthropological study, but she has drawn on a large number of other Chinese works as well.

39. Ibid., 145–150.

40. Ibid., 153–154.

41. Ibid., 12.

42. Ibid., 229.

43. Ibid., 9, 221.

44. Laurence A. Schneider, *A Madman of Ch'u: The Chinese Myth of Loyalty and Dissent* (Berkeley, 1980), 76–77, on Chu Hsi; 1, 3, on out-line of Ch'ü Yüan's biography.

45. According to Schneider (*Madman,* 27), the primary Chinese source is a collection of Ch'ü Yüan's writings put together by one Wang I (fl. A.D. 110–120, or roughly four centuries after the author's death). This text is the starting point for subsequent centuries of discussion by

Chinese scholar-officials. An English translation, endorsed by a Chinese scholar, appeared in 1929: Lim Boon Keng, trans., *The Li Sao: An Elegy on Encountering Sorrows* (Shanghai, 1929). References below in Roman numerals refer to stanzas, in Arabic numerals to individual lines.

46. See *Li Sao,* 40, where "She" refers to the absent king; also lines 17–24 and others.

47. *Li Sao,* notes and commentaries, 129. See also p. 130 on lines 71–74.

48. Thomas A. Metzger, *Escape From Predicament: Neo-Confucianism and China's Evolving Political Culture* (New York, 1977), made an important contribution by documenting this severe strain on the scholar-official.

49. See *Chinese Tradition,* 1:514–516, for useful introductory remarks; 516–522 for the text of Wang Yang-ming's "Inquiry on the Great Learning" and other statements.

50. Ibid., 1:517.

51. Ibid., 1:518; see also 520.

52. Ibid., 1:518–519.

53. Ibid., 1:525.

* Index *

Aaron, brother of Moses, 11, 14
abominations: idolatry as, 11; Old
    Testament listing of, 8–9
"About the Persons Incarcerated"
    speech (Saint-Just, 1794), 80–81
Adam and Eve, 37
adultery prohibition, 5, 7
afterlife beliefs, 31–32
Amita Buddha, 112
Anabaptists revolt of 1535 (Münster),
    31
Analects (Confucius), 120–121
the Ark, 101
atonement, 22
avoidance rules, 16

bestiality prohibition, 8–9, 17
Bèze, Theodore de, 42, 43
blood shedding, 19
bodhisattvas, 110, 111, 112, 114, 115.
    See also Buddhism
Book of Leviticus: on idolatry and
    sexuality, 4, 8, 9; listing unclean ob-
    jects, 13–14; on the rules of sacri-
    fice, 13–14. *See also* Old Testament
Brahmins (priests), 105
Brissot, Jacques-Pierre, 61, 62
Buddhism: Chinese persecution
    against, 117–118; criminal behav-
    ior under, 113; moral purity con-
    cept within, 108–110, 111–113,
    115; origins/nonpersecuting doc-
    trine of, 109–110, 132, 149n.30;
    Pure Land sect of, 110, 111–112;
    spread to China, 110; unclean
    things under, 113
Buddhism of the Elders (Theravada
    Buddhism), 109, 115
Burckhardt, Jacob, 26

Calvin, John: on concept of purity,
    36–37; influence of writings by,

28; rise of as Huguenot movement
    leader, 36; theocratic utopia of, 33
Calvinism: Catholic expressions on,
    39–43; comparison of Catholic
    faith and, 31–33; converts to, 33–
    34; denial of Catholicism by, 30,
    34–35; doctrine offered by, 34–35;
    predestination doctrine of, 37–38;
    on salvation through faith, 38–39;
    theocratic utopia of, 33. *See also*
    Huguenots
Calvinists: accusations against
    Catholic Church by, 44–45; simi-
    larities of ancient Hebrews and,
    56–58. *See also* Huguenots
cardinal de Tournon, 42
Carnival in Romans revolt (1580),
    49, 52–55
Catherine de Medici, Queen Mother
    (France), 42, 49–50, 51
Catherine the Great, Empress (Rus-
    sia), 103–104
Catholic Church. *See* French
    Catholic Church
Champagne province (France),
    31–32, 33–34
Charles IX, King (France), 42,
    49–50, 51
childbirth impurities, 18–19
Ch'in dynasty (China), 116–117
China: Ch'ü Yüan legend of predy-
    nastic, 124–126, 149n.45; first
    emperor of, 116–117; Neo-
    Confucianism of, 122–123, 124,
    126; revolutionary purity of Cul-
    tural Revolution in, 132. *See also*
    Confucian China
Chinese Legalists, 94
Chinese Tradition (Chu Hsi), 122
Ch'ing dynasty (China), 118
Christianity: Hebrew intolerance in-
    herited by, 26; Hebrew legacy to,

151

speech (Saint-Just, 1793), 78, 80–82, 83
Four Noble Truths (Buddhism), 109
"Fragments" (Saint-Just), 97
France: Carnival in Romans revolt (1580) in, 49, 52–55; food riots (1792) in, 70; Massacre of St. Bartholomew's Day (1572) in, 48–52, 54–55, 130; rationalist thought of eighteenth century in, 102; rebellion against revolutionary rule in, 84; religious cleavage within, 39–48; religious war expanded to class war in, 48–55; similarities of ancient Hebrews and sixteenth century, 56–58; Wars of Religion in, 43, 56–63, 131
free choice, 36–37
French Catholic Church: clerical abuses within, 28–29, 139n.31; compared with Huguenot faith, 31–33; early reform attempts by, 28–29; Huguenot accusations against, 44–48; official opinions on Huguenots by, 39–43; similarities of ancient Hebrews and, 56–58; treatment for guilt by, 32
French National Church synod (1561), 41–42
French Protestant identity, 33, 35. See also Calvinism; Huguenots
French Revolution: disintegration of radical revolutionary leadership of, 96–97; food riots (1792) following, 70; the Girondins of the, 61–62, 69, 71, 76, 142n.9; the guillotine as remedy to weaknesses of, 67; Hébert on purity and radicalism of, 63–67; moral purity issue of, 62–63, 71–74, 131–132; rationalist movement/militant monotheism of, 102–103; revolutionary purity as legacy of, 132; Robespierre on popular support for, 72–73; Robespierre on purity and

revolutionary radicalism of, 68–78; Saint-Just on failures of the, 97–100; Saint-Just on purity and revolutionary radicalism of, 76–100; use of guillotine during, 66–67, 98, 104. See also Committee of Public Safety
French Revolution (Doyle) [Oxford, 1989], 91

Galpern, Aubrey, 33, 35
the Girondins, 61–62, 69, 71, 76, 142n.9
God's judgments, 37–38
golden calf idolatry, 11–12, 130
Goldhagen, Daniel, 58
the guillotine, 66–67, 98, 104. See also terror
guilt-control, 32

Harijans. See Untouchables
Hébert, Marie-Jean: execution of, 71, 89, 90; on purity and revolutionary radicalism, 63–67
Hebrews: dietary restrictions of, 16, 23–24, 136n.11; monotheism legacy of, 25–26, 129–130; morality as mores of, 23–24; Old Testament on rewards given to, 101; siege mentality of, 18; similarities of sixteenth-century French and, 56–58; terroristic theocracy of the, 25
"Hell of Uninterrupted Suffering" (Buddhism), 113
Heller, Henry, 48, 50, 54
Henri IV, King (France), 63
Henry II, King (France), 31
Henry III, King (France), 41
Henry of Navarre (later Henry IV), 42, 49
d'Herbois, Collot, 95
heresy, 131. See also the Reform
Herodotus, 67
Hindu caste system, 105–106, 109, 132